THE ART OF SCHOOLING
FOR DRESSAGE

The author in complete balance in passage on Pedro

THE ART OF SCHOOLING FOR DRESSAGE

A CLASSICAL APPROACH

Sylvia Stanier

S P

Copyright © 2005 Sylvia Stanier

The right of Sylvia Stanier to be identified as the author of this work has been asserted in accordance with the Copyright, Design and Patent Act 1988

First published in the UK in 2005
by The Sportsman's Press, an imprint of Quiller Publishing Ltd
Line drawings by Maggie Raynor

British Library Cataloguing-in-Publication Data
A catalogue record for this book
is available from the British Library

ISBN 1 904057 69 1

Printed in Singapore

The Sportsman's Press

An imprint of Quiller Publishing Ltd
Wykey House, Wykey, Shrewsbury, SY4 1JA
Tel: 01939 261616 Fax: 01939 261606
E-mail: info@quillerbooks.com
Website: www.swanhillbooks.com

ACKNOWLEDGEMENTS

I wish to thank Susan McBane for her help and editorial expertise in producing this book.

The line drawings are all by Maggie Raynor; a few of them appeared in my previous books *The Art of Long Reining* and *The Art of Lungeing* and are reproduced by kind permission of the Publishers, J A Allen.

The photographs are by John Evans, Fiona Forbes, Charles Fennell and Kit Houghton, and are credited accordingly.

Sylvia Stanier,
Northamptonshire
Summer 2005

CONTENTS

INTRODUCTION

Before reading the text of this book I think it is important that the reader studies this introduction. It is easy to write down the aids for the various movements, but that means taking many things out of context.

I am a great believer in bonding and partnership between horse and rider, whilst retaining the basic principles of 'horse sense'. Being kind to a horse does not only mean giving 'tit-bits' for no particular reason. Horses do not think as humans, but as horses. Some humans are more sensitive than others – they feel things more easily or get upset more easily. Horses are the same; on some you only have to think and they respond, others have to have things spelled out one foot at a time. The aids laid down in this book are logical and should work if applied with care and clarity.

My own teachers were Colonel Joe Hume Dudgeon, who was very wise and humane, and Einar Schmit Jensen, who was a very patient man, who said he simply explained to the horse (aid-wise) what to do – very slowly and with no fuss – which is easier said than done! Another person who had an influence on my riding early on was Sam Marsh, the great show hack trainer, whose aim was to produce horses which were light in hand and a pleasure to look at.

My aim has always been to produce horses which, to use an old Army

Working with the Master; Einar Schmit Jensen on Yuba.
(ABOVE) *with an extended outline and* (BELOW) *with a collected outline*

saying, 'showed maximum effect with minimal effort'. Therefore it is important to realise that however direct the written aid may be, it is the interpretation towards 'lightness' that should always be the aim.

Maestro Nuno Oliveira brought 'lightness' to a very high art. I feel lucky to have studied with him and to have ridden and felt horses in the highest forms of collection, in self-balance and completely light to the aids.

Obviously when you start out on this road it will take time and practice. A stronger aid or more definite position may be necessary for the horse to begin with but then lessen everything bit by bit until it is happening automatically. But then again it may be necessary to have less aid or position to begin with – that is the problem of training, there is no one answer. To ask too much can lead to trouble and asking too little is not much good either.

I have tried to explain the movements and the aids logically in this book – that is with a progression that horses will accept. For instance, it is easier for the horse to learn a shoulder-in before learning the half-pass, and he must learn to obey the rider's leg aid, particularly moving away from it before doing *any* lateral work, and before that he must learn to go forward from the rider's leg aid.

Horses vary so much and the easiest horse I ever had to break in was a little horse called 'Finn'. I followed the Army notes and had him riding in six weeks and out hunting after eight weeks, he competed at Badminton and lived until he was twenty-eight. His full sister, 'Fru', was the exact opposite and it took two people to hold the lunge line when we put the roller on; she later went on to become an international show jumper, after a successful career as an Irish international show jumper.

One of the things to understand is how to assess your horse, and if it is possible to help the problems, or correct them. I hope this book will be useful, and that readers will gain good results from it.

1.
WHAT IS DRESSAGE?

When one thinks of dressage, the immediate thought is of the Lipizzaners from Vienna, the Cadre Noir from Saumur, or a High School horse in the circus. These are spectacular displays with expert riders performing very difficult movements with ease. This is a wonderful picture to have in one's mind, but to achieve this level is a lifetime's work. However there is no reason why one should not be able to have a great deal of fun at a lower level.

The word 'dressage' is much mis-used. It comes from the French word 'dresser', which means 'to dress', that is to put the finishing touches to something. So to 'dress' your horse you need to improve his way of going and that is by giving him further training. This is where confusion first arises because to 'school' a horse basically is one thing, and very important too, but to teach him dressage is different, although the one emanates from the other.

From basic schooling there are many outlets – show jumping, eventing, endurance and showing to name but a few. I think it would be fair to say 'Pure Dressage' starts at the upper Novice Level – if one counts Novice as being part of basic schooling. Of course some specialist trainers start with the idea that the horse is going to be a dressage horse and that's that. However, if the horse has achieved a good Novice standard, he can then

Fanny, winner of the Irish Dressage Championships 1967, ridden by the author

progress up the ladder according to his ability.

What of the rider?

If the rider already has knowledge of the aids, then further study of these in depth is the order of the day. However, for someone who has ridden all their lives but not studied dressage then an immediate study of the subject is essential, starting at the very beginning. This is not with the idea of making dressage so difficult that one doesn't wish to go on. It is to clarify the subject and make it easier.

Although one expects good riders to integrate with their horses, this can best be achieved by a study of the subject theoretically and by physical practice, i.e. riding.

The rider should try and learn the terminology and the layout of a dressage arena. Most importantly of all he/she should learn the basic aids – that is the uses of the legs, the hands, and the body-weight. This can be done by reading books or looking at videos but the question of balance and rhythm must be felt and practised on a horse.

To begin with the time lag between the rider asking for a movement and the horse responding will be quite slow. This time lag will shorten as the reflexes in both horse and rider are developed.

One of the biggest differences between a cross-country horse, or in some cases a show jumper and a dressage horse, is that the dressage horse must wait until asked to do something by his rider, whereas the cross-country, and often the show jumping horse retains a certain amount of his own initiative.

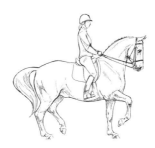

Michael Page on Pan American and Olympic medal winner Grasshopper riding in the French style

2.
ASSESSMENT AND FAULTS

When evaluating a horse's work, I find the F.E.I. scale of marks extremely useful, 0 to 10 with the remarks beside each number. However, that doesn't tell you the specific fault. You, the judge or trainer have to decide why or what the fault is and how serious and whether it can be corrected. The F.E.I. Rule Book is very specific in what is required, but it is up to the trainer or rider to decide on what to do when something is occurring that is *not* required: a big and controversial subject.

I have two criteria by which I try to assess a horse, one is is he in 'self-balance' and two is he elastic and gymnastic? Obviously a horse that is very excitable can cause problems and so can one that won't go forwards.

In this book I have set out a set of aids and have tried to explain that the goal should always be towards lightness. When taking a lesson I always like to assess the horse and rider, and try and pinpoint the most important fault. This very often focuses on lack of balance or stiffness in either horse or rider. If one is riding oneself, you have to try and feel what is wrong.

Some people look to see if a horse's mouth is working correctly and by that I mean closed with a little bit of lather showing. If the horse is 'mouthing' properly then he is probably relaxed all through his body (and mind) and is therefore working correctly.

A 'wrong bend' in any pace means a loss of balance and stiffness throughout, 'over-bending' means too much weight on the shoulders and forehand leading to the inability to collect properly. The hind legs are not able to carry the weight properly when the balance goes onto the hind quarters.

A horse that has a 'wrong bend' needs to work on a large circle with contact on the *outside* rein to allow the *inside* hind leg to become more active and work under the horse, gradually the neck will become more flexible, especially with some vibration of the *inside* rein.

Much the same can be said of 'over-bending' but with ever more emphasis on the outside rein to allow the freeing of the inside shoulder which will throw the weight onto the outside shoulder and the balance much further back.

The use of the rider's hands should be clear but never rough, and the rider's legs must be doing more than the hands so that the horse is, so to speak, in front of the rider's legs. These are probably the most important faults, from which most other faults emanate.

Problems such as not tracking-up, hollow back, tilting of the head, unsteady or open mouth are all nearly always the product of stiffness or over-bending. Sometimes, pain or ill-fitting tack contribute, also sharp teeth particularly 'wolf-teeth' which can be very uncomfortable.

In the walk 'pacing' – that is walking in a lateral gait – is a basic fault. It may be because of stiffness in the horse's back, or trying to make the horse walk too fast. A good 'swing' of his hind legs is necessary for a good walk.

In the trot, it may not be generally known that a horse cannot put his foot on the ground beyond his muzzle. So the use of the horse's shoulders is essential for a correct trot. The low 'pointing of the toe' trot, although spectacular, if not accompanied by good shoulder movement is in fact not entirely correct. Work at walk and trot over poles on the ground can help here as can trotting on a long rein, to encourage shoulder movement.

In the canter, apart from wrong leads and general stiffness the most usual fault is cantering in four time instead of three time. Some horses may try and do this naturally, especially the Iberians. In this case the horse should be asked to extend the canter so as to loosen his back muscles and increase impulsion, and only asked to collect for a few paces at a time until he has got out of the habit. These horses often try to use the four time beat to keep their balance in the canter pirouette – or they may try and rush round as fast as they can, also to keep their balance. Practise the pirouette on a slightly larger circle to try and establish confidence and calmness, before coming in close.

In high collection horses often take uneven steps and this may be a rider error in over-riding (unless the horse has a back problem). Try then to maintain the balance and collection with a little less aid. Maybe less hand, or not quite so much leg. I have had horses who once into high collection, like to get on with things and only require me to sit in balance, i.e. to lessen (but not drop) the aid.

This latter criteria works especially well in the lateral movements. I think of Nuno Oliveira's phrase, 'give the horse the position, give him the aid, and then let the horse do the movement'. It is amazing how that works!

*It is important to establish a good bond between horse and rider. The author with the
Arabian stallion Hussein – an intelligent horse who bonded well with his handler*

3.
THE THEME

In every walk of life progress is achieved from basic principles. Equitation has benefited from new techniques based on old ones, especially in veterinary science, feeding, saddlery and training methods. Whether one looks at the Spanish Riding School in Vienna, the French riders at Saumur or the German riders at Warendorf, each school has its own agenda based on very solid foundations laid down by the 'Masters'. These principles have stood the test of time. There is a saying that you cannot have a tree without a trunk, the branches growing out of that trunk thus using the product of the base. Both horse and rider must learn, and become established in the basics, before trying to specialise in a particular discipline. This attitude was firmly instilled into me by my trainers.

How then does one establish things? My first thought is that the horses must have system (which must be flexible) based on sound principles. Flexibility means taking into account such things as a horse's age, its conformation and temperament. Equally so the rider's age, shape and ability.

Explanation, Demonstration, Implementation, Equitation. Explain what you want, demonstrate how to do it, ask the pupil to implement the movement, discuss it and ask the pupil to repeat the exercise. This sequence works just the same with horses. The trainer must arrange the horse so that the horse is mentally as well as physically able to perform the movement required. Once performed, slow down or stop, reward the horse if appropriate. Then perform the movement again to establish it in the horse's mind.

The success or failure of a movement is usually contained in the preparation. Organise the horse, arrange his position and pace. Preparation is just as important in jumping as it is in dressage – more so probably. The horse has a small brain which panics easily (especially if a Thoroughbred) and like an elephant he never forgets, in fact he cannot. De-fusing a situation is therefore imperative.

The theme must be quietly firm whilst remaining humane. Use minimum effort to obtain maximum result. The effort may have to be more in the beginning, the aids being reduced as and where possible, always looking for the 'Lightness'. When rewarding or correcting a horse this must be done instantaneously so that he connects either with the immediate circumstances.

In my library I have divided my books into sections dealing with the various systems of equitation – German, French, Scandinavian, etc. This gives me an opportunity to 'keep familiar' with the different systems and to look things up. I also keep my veterinary books together for easy access. One is constantly updating one's mind, to see if there are improvements within the original guidelines which should be considered.

The best way to study a system is to learn it – like a foreign language – but that is not always possible. Watching good riders who adhere to their National School's principles is a good way to learn without much trouble. Watch good exponents of French equitation by watching their jumping riders or their dressage riders, who probably emanate from Saumur. The top German riders will show the training used at Warendorf. The riders from Vienna are steeped in their own traditions.

The eye is the window to the brain – don't be afraid to use it – find out what suits you and your horse and keep to it.

4.
THE RIDER

Introduction to Balance

To start with you do not need a fancy schoolmaster, in fact it is easier to learn on a nice quiet school horse, where there is no tension and mistakes may be made without troubles arising.

Learning to sit straight in the saddle at the halt, and learning to relax and feel the movement of the horse at walk and later at slow trot are primary requirements. The horse may even be on the lunge line giving the rider the space and time to feel. Once this feel has been established you have the first sign of integrating with the horse. To establish balance the rider does not use the reins and learns to stand in the stirrups without straightening or setting the knee joint. If the knee is set and straight the rider's body is set too, and out of balance. When the knee is slightly bent the rider's weight flows down to the ankle joint and onto the ball of the foot. This is the focal pivot and support. The upper body is very slightly forward. Although this position is not maintained throughout dressage training, it is the key position for finding the horse's point of balance. In order to influence the horse's higher training in collection and extension it is crucial to feel and to alter at will, that balance.

If a rider is young and supple then he/she should find this position of balance easy. Older riders with stiff muscles and maybe old injuries will take

*Stirrup leather too long. The rider's foot
not correctly placed in the stirrup*

This rider is leaning too far back

a little longer. Muscles have to be re-organised. This may often be best attained by doing some exercises at home. Some of course can be performed on the horse. The teacher must be sympathetic and beware of unsafe exercises and situations. In other words, I am saying physiotherapy on horseback is the way to loosen your muscles up. Remember however, not to ask too much too soon or the rider will become very sore!

To help muscles soften up, older riders may find a course of massage helpful, whilst others who are trying to convert fat into muscles that will become supple enough for dressage riding will find a diet change to health foods useful.

Explaining the rider's position (JOHN EVANS)

The circulation comes into the rider's department as well as the horse's; it is only by getting one's whole body working with the blood circulating throughout that one can truly work the muscles and become supple. Do not confuse developing muscles for strength, but think of it more as being flexible like a ballet dancer. Dressage is not about strength, but about tact.

The Mental Side

As well as being physically good for one, dressage should also be mentally good for one.

Dressage riding certainly stimulates the brain because one has to use it to think clearly. It also improves self-discipline in that dressage is, or should be, an orderly affair. Calmness in both horse and rider are paramount. If a horse is frightened it cannot think, and if the rider is in a state of panic there can be no clearness of thought.

Many riders are apt to confuse calmness with the horse doing nothing at all. They seem hesitant to use the aids for fear of upsetting or hurting their horse. Confidence in one's own sense of ability is important – not arrogance, but a proper knowledge of the subject.

Horses that have had a bad experience will often never forget it. They may be helped to a degree, but one cannot ever completely erase that experience. The same goes for a rider. If someone has had a bad fall – or been scared by a horse for some reason – this may be overcome to a large extent because one can talk about it.

I believe the easiest way for the learning process to succeed is by teaching at the slower paces, halt and walk. Explanations may need to be repeated time after time until the rider suddenly indicates they at last understand.

The separate control of limbs is part physical and part mental. Like reflexes this will take time to develop and it is part of learning dressage. There are many aids that involve using one hand or one leg in a different way from the opposite one.

Something many riders find difficult to understand is applying the leg aids alternately, this is because they do not have independent control of their limbs. An example of this would be when applying one leg near the girth and the other behind it. This action must be thought out first, then applied and finally it will need very little thought and become a reflex – it will probably take about twenty lessons. The brain must work with the muscles, and the muscles must be made ready, through suppleness to work with the brain.

One of the first exercises to encourage separate control of limbs is to ride with the reins in one hand and doing other things with the free hand – for example such as swinging the arm forward and back or rotating it, whilst keeping the rein hand steady. The same applies to the legs: keep one steady and swing the other one backwards and forwards. Do this for eight or ten goes at a time.

Over Concentration and Tension

Often an inexperienced rider will try too hard, thus causing stiffness and tension. Little things such as holding one's breath inadvertently, setting one's jaw, setting of tight wrists and ankles are signs of anxiety. The wish to succeed goes too far. It causes one to grip too tightly, and leads to hard contact on the reins. A teacher may say 'Relax' but often the best thing to do is to stop the horse and rider and at the halt explain the problem. Try and get the rider to smile or even talk about something else. Then try again doing less, not more, to make the horse respond.

Of course there should be a partnership in all the disciplines, and as the trained dressage horse has to be so obedient, this illustrates the need for the dressage rider to learn the aids correctly. Once

A rider showing tension

these are learned then it is a matter of applying them – the learning may be theoretical, but the application is an art. The aids must be applied clearly and in the correct place, as lightly as possible with maximum effect.

Creating the best situation (or dealing with a bad one sometimes) is important too. Creating the correct amount of energy so as to produce the best movement from the horse needs to be felt practically, and each horse will be different. Putting the horse in 'position' is part of the proceedings. So a study of a horse's conformation and psychology will help the rider to solve problems.

If the psychology of the horse is not understood, then a good partnership will be very difficult to achieve. This is where riders, in desperation, try to dominate their horses by force. Of all the disciplines dressage should be carried out elegantly.

Bonding

Bonding is a very popular word, but what does it actually mean? If you can feel what your horse is doing underneath you, then you are well on the way – you need that sort of feel. Monty Roberts has brought bonding to a very high level, and rightly so. What I am concerned with is the long-term bonding. They say a dog is man's best friend and I agree, but the horse is equally so.

Bonding is not simply giving your horse tit-bits, but rather the creation of a partnership. The horse should respect his master as would a child his parent. Make friends with your horse through reward – a pat, or possibly a piece of carrot or a horse nut. I would advise you to be careful giving sugar, especially to colts, as it can lead to biting.

When working from the ground eye contact is the key. The use of the voice and the body movements are all part and parcel of the bonding process. The horse will learn your voice quickly and also what your body movements mean. When lungeing for instance, if you go towards your horse and hold your hand up, he will soon learn to stop. If you are consistent he will learn to trust you and obey. We have all been using this method for years but have not put a name to it. What I am advocating is not exactly what Monty Roberts teaches with advance and retreat but it's not far off it. The British Army Manual has a saying, 'it is only the man who really loves his horse who can gain the most from his horse'.

Some Exercises

I like to start off a lesson (unless someone has asked for a specific subject, in which case I expect horse and rider to be 'worked-in'), with physical exercises. Starting at the extremities, the toes and the fingers and working-in towards the main body. I recommend doing these for ten minutes before proceeding to the balance exercises which may overlap followed by a few minutes on the aids. Later on, say in a month or approximately twenty lessons, when the pupil understands the work, then one can lessen the exercise time so as to progress to learn certain movements, and the transitions.

Foot and leg exercises (*without stirrups*)

Toes down
Toes up
Swinging lower leg backwards and forwards
Rotating ankle joints

Arm and hand exercises

Playing with fingers – opening and folding them
Clenching and un-clenching hands
Rotating wrists
Flexing wrists outwards and inwards
Rotating shoulders with arms going
   forward, up, back and down slowly

Head and neck exercises

Turning neck and head to the right and left

New Technology

In the realms of sports technology I believe that three things (or four if you include massage for humans as well as horses) are relevant. One is the video as a teaching aid. It can be useful to have one's lesson videoed and then study it at home or with the teacher. Some people feel a need for a sports psychologist and I think they can be helpful to instil confidence in the rider before a big competition and also to improve concentration.

Concentrated dressage training is akin to gymnastics and muscles, especially in horses, can get damaged. There are many good horse chiropractors nowadays, some even work with people as well. They must be qualified practitioners. Veterinary surgeons will usually give the necessary permission and release information regarding the horse's previous problems, but by law must be consulted.

Watching videos of famous riders is a very good way of learning, especially if there is a good commentary.

5.
THE HORSE'S FRAME

The Structure

To obtain the best results from your horse not only is it important to know what you want but also how best to achieve that result. Knowing which muscles and ligaments do what is essential.

Tendons connect muscle to bone, whereas ligaments connect bone to bone. Both tendons and ligaments have little circulation hence when damaged they lose elasticity and do not mend easily.

The horse is said to balance himself by his use of his head and neck. The horse's head is extremely heavy in relation to the rest of his body and is carried

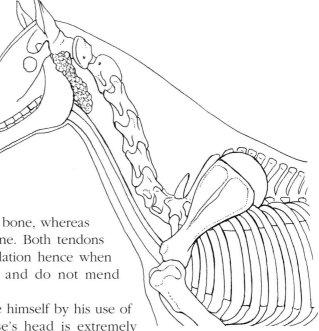

The horse's neck

The neck, back and stomach muscles of the horse

at the end of the neck which is flexible. There are seven vertebrae (cervical) in the neck. These vertebrae allow the horse to turn his head and neck as well as to move it up and down. The head is held in position by very strong muscle situated at the top of the poll and forming the top of the horse's neck going into the withers.

It is a point of training that these 'crest' muscles should be worked to develop them to the maximum. To develop, muscles need good circulation, by stretching and contracting these muscles they should develop, and be able to carry the horse's head either in high collection or for jumping.

Much has been written about horses' backs. The area from the withers to the croup is vulnerable to injury. Due to the structure of the horse's back it is not easy to mend any damage. The back connects the front and hind ends. It is not actually meant for sitting on, but man has managed to domesticate the horse by sitting on him. It is therefore a good idea to find the place on the horse's back where he can carry the rider most easily. Usually this is just behind the withers, behind the cervical and thoracic muscles. The dorsal muscles under the 'saddle' area are long and thin and

This horse has a good strong back. The back is slightly long and the withers are reasonably high (JOHN EVANS)

do not have much flexibility, the vertebrae (the thoracic and lumbar) are often close together at their tips. Damage often occurs in this area, particularly with a long saddle or as a result of too much of the rider's weight.

The lumbar muscles are prone to damage and should not be overloaded (either with a long saddle or from the rider's weight). The ligaments which hold these vertebrae together are very strong but once damaged they are extremely difficult to mend. The muscles, which come from the spine down over the ribs, make a good cushion for the saddle to sit on. This is where the rider's weight can be best accommodated. A very short back will have short thick ligaments and a long-backed horse thin ligaments – each carries difficulties.The muscles surrounding the ribs stretch and contract as the horse moves.

The horse's tail is used to remove flies, and is also an important element of balance. The tail is part of the series of vertebrae working from the poll, neck, back and quarters. A horse trainer can see if a horse is 'using his back' by watching the tail. If the horse swings his tail in a relaxed manner from

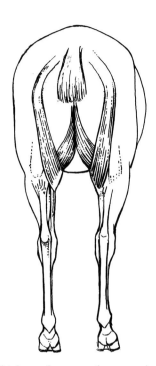 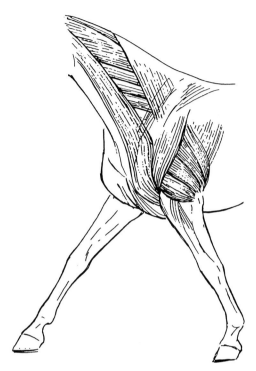

Thighs and quarters (BACK VIEW)   *Shoulders and neck*

side to side it is almost certain that the ligaments in the loin area will be relaxed. These ligaments and the muscles in that area will appear soft and rippling as opposed to hard and set. This is known as the 'swing' of the back. A horse will clamp his tail down if he is going to go backwards and he will carry it out horizontally when galloping. When rearing a horse will carry his tail out to balance himself. The horse carries his tail over his back when very excited or alarmed. In this case the tail is a signal to other horses that all is not well.

A saddle which is placed on top of the withers area can easily damage the median nerves which are situated at the bottom of the shoulder blade.The angle of the shoulders is an indication of what sort of action a horse will have. A long, sloping shoulder will give a long stride and, if well set into, a long wither, will be comfortable to sit on. The humerus bone, which should be reasonably long and well laid, indicates the ability to raise the shoulder and forehand when training. An upright humerus indicates poor action and a heavy front.

A long muscular fore-arm, together with a good shoulder should provide a long stride in a trot and in gallop. Short cannon bones with big knees provide strength to carry the heavy weight of the shoulders and ribs. The pasterns should, like the shoulders, be well angled, not too long and weak, or too upright and inflexible (uncomfortable).

A Thoroughbred of 16.h.h. weighs approximately 1200 to 1500 lb, so when in full gallop – or leaping over a fence – approximately nine-tenths of that weight can be put on one front leg for a split second. This is the moment when the tendons around the cannon bone can give way, known as 'breaking down'.

The hind limbs of the horse are complex – although some of the bones are similar to those of a front leg. The hock joint is used both to elevate and to propel the hind quarters. Where a horse has a very straight hock joint it will have great propelling power, but although like a pole vault, it can push upwards, a straight hock does not always have the capacity to flex the pelvic point of hip and hip joints (via the stifle joints) as required in Advanced dressage. The development of the inner thigh (second thigh) muscles helps the strength of the whole hind leg. It is the big quarter muscles, the biceps and triceps, which really propel the horse, and which in the dressage horse have to carry the weight transferred from the forehand. Muscles used to propel work horizontally, those carrying work vertically. It is only by working the horse consistently through the various collecting and extending movements, that the horse learns to adapt his muscles, just as a human athlete does. Watching a highly collected horse working (in passage for instance), all the joints of the legs will be flexing up and down working vertically (i.e. carrying), whilst still retaining the ability to propel. Make sure the hind legs are propelling forwards, but once into high collection the 'tracking up' will be less so when the carrying effect comes into play, the impulsion being contained within the horse's balance. The hind legs need to adjust more than the front ones to go into carrying mode.

Hind legs and quarters

The large quarter muscles and the ligaments of the back work in different ways in trot and in canter. The back ligaments have to loosen and work more when in canter. It is a good idea therefore to do work at the trot (circles) and then do the same movement in canter, so that all muscles are worked.

Horses with narrow chests are difficult to balance, but can perform the lateral movements quite easily. Horses which have good width between each point of the hip are usually powerful, and can balance well, but find the crossing over of the front legs more difficult. One really has to work on what is there and improve what is possible to improve within reason.

Muscles which are worked hard are vulnerable to damage, i.e. bruising or strain. To help keep muscles in good order, judicious massage is recommended. Massage helps the circulation, and is essential in promoting healing when damage has occurred.

Areas where extra strain is put on muscles vary according to the discipline to be performed and the following is a guide to areas which benefit from massage:

Dressage: The muscles at the top of the poll, also particularly those around the withers and the loins (behind and under the saddle), the large muscles. Flexors of the hind quarters and gaskins as well as the abductors and adductors of the front and hind limbs. The shoulder muscles and the chest (pectoral) muscles together with the muscles of the forearms.

Show Jumping: All the muscles running down the back of the quarters and the gaskins. The abductors and adductors of the front and hind limbs. The loins just behind and under the saddles. The chest and elbows.

Cross-Country: The same as for show jumping, but the whole shoulder area should be included because of the extra speed and stretch required from the horse. The top of the horse's back is also at risk due to the extra propulsion and stretching.

Hill Work: This is useful for a number of reasons:

a) As a fittening exercise. Walking or cantering up easy gradients for distances of half to one mile opens the lungs and also stretches the quarter and shoulder muscles.

b) It improves the use of quarter muscles. Walk the horse up fairly steep gradients (approximately one quarter of a mile). Do not trot or canter the horse up steep slopes as this can damage the hocks.

c) It improves the use of shoulder muscles. Walk the horse down fairly steep gradients (approximately one quarter of a mile). Do not trot or canter the horse down steep slopes, as this can damage the tendons of the front legs, and jar the shoulders.

The Head and Jaw

The shape of the horse's head has a considerable bearing on how the horse responds to training.

A horse with a big heavy head or a thick neck will be likely to have trouble bringing weight off his forehand. A horse with a small head can sometimes have a long thin neck which can contain flexing problems.

The width of the jaw bones can give notice of problems. Very narrow jaw bones mean the bars of the mouth and the tongue are apt to become pinched. The bit is thus uncomfortable. The windpipe and the salivary

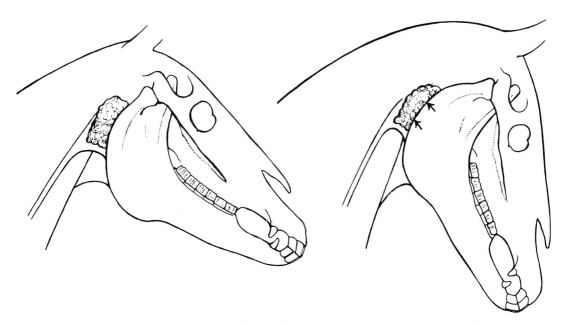

In some horses, conformation of the jaw bone can cause compression of the salivary glands when the horse is collected

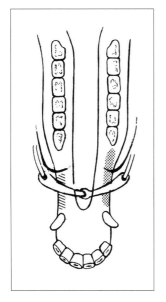

A horse's jaw, showing correct fitting of snaffle

glands also become pinched by the big round bones at the neck end. The inhalation of air is also constricted. Possibly one of the least considered points of the jaw bones is the inner edges. These can be either wide and smooth or narrow and rough. This roughness interferes with the salivary glands and prevents them expanding between the end of the neck and the jaw bones. This means the horse will find it uncomfortable to flex properly. The old fashioned test of the width of a man's fist should fit between the jaw bones is a good indication. At the same time, run a finger along the jaw bones.

Instincts, Senses and the Weather

Having set out the general principles, this seems an appropriate time to talk about creating a 'rapport' with your horse and to consider certain problems a rider may encounter along the way.

Understanding your horse's instincts as well as his senses make for a better 'rapport'. The horse's natural instincts are: Fear of Pain and Pain itself; Finding Food and Water. He is a gregarious or herd animal. He panics if left alone or when parted from another. Panic sets in very easily due to the horse's small brain and his natural instinct to flee. Natural instincts can be curbed to some extent when thoroughly domesticated and by good understanding. A domesticated horse has a great capacity to please and responds well to rewards, but will take advantage if petted too much. There should be mutual respect between a man and his horse. As the British Cavalry Manual says, 'only a man who loves and understands his horse will achieve the best from his horse'.

The senses are: Smell, Eyesight, Hearing and Memory. All of these senses can be made use of by the rider or trainer.

When observing a horse in the stable or at grass, notice that he will first of all look at you; if frightened of you or a dog or some other distraction, he may raise his head and snort and move away from you. His instinct is to flee whatever he perceives to be danger. If he is not frightened he will come up to you and sniff you to see if there is no danger and to see if you have a reward for him.

The horse uses his ears – backwards and forwards, or pricked right forward, ready to react quickly.

The eyes are exceptionally wide-angled and can see to the side and often behind as well. Remember horses' senses are more acutely developed than those of humans.

Memory is very clear to a horse and once a habit is learned it is almost impossible to completely eradicate it. Sadly bad habits are often learned quicker than good ones. It is only when we understand these things that we can mould the horse into what we would like him to be. 'A trained horse is one that responds rightly, lightly and with energy to his trainer's commands' (Cavalry Manual).

Horses like routine – it is easier for them to remember. Try and feed horses at the same time each day, and also try and exercise at the same time of day. Keep to the routine of your training schedule, but when hacking out, which should be a relaxation for all concerned, vary the route, otherwise a clever horse may soon decide which route he prefers and not to go on any other.

Problems which may occur when a horse does not respond, or responds badly when being schooled, are often caused by stiffness and/or stiffness in the rider. A stiff horse may not bend properly on a circle or may lead with the wrong leg in canter. Stiffness in the muscles of the horse's back and hind quarters causes loss of balance.

Equally, one may be asking too much too soon. A rider who is stiff in his/her back will also cause problems for the horse. Stiff arms and wrists are a cause of mouth problems. An unsuitable place or situation may cause a horse to lose concentration. Sometimes a horse becomes fractious if something is hurting him – it might be a sore mouth or tooth, a leg or foot injury, a sore back or badly fitting saddlery.

Praise and reward your horse for doing well but do not punish him when he has failed to perform a movement well. Possibly he has not understood – patience is very much a virtue. It is better to stop a lesson early if the horse has performed what you wanted. Try and finish on a good note.

Weather Effects

As to the weather, in competitions horses are expected to accept all conditions. However, nice calm conditions make life easier. Good conditions underfoot are always better than slippery ones. Some horses prefer soft ground, especially those with high knee action when galloping, others prefer drier ground. That is one aspect of weather, and other effects a trainer should concern himself with are rain, wind and temperature. Rain, especially cold rain, is uncomfortable for both horse and rider when training, but it can be quite exhilarating to ride in when out hunting. Slippery conditions when training distract and frighten a horse. So an indoor or outdoor training area with a good surface is essential. It need not be enormous, 40 x 60 metres is enough. Nowadays it is very easy to hire an arena locally for an hour or so. Windy conditions upset horses, often making them nervy. Leaves or other things blowing about surprise them. Very hot conditions make horses lazy and cause them to sweat, and they tend to shake and rub as a result. In very hot climates people tend to ride early in the morning or in the evening to avoid the heat. Very cold conditions tend to make horses awkward. They come with hard, tense back and neck muscles, and will not concentrate.

So do look at the sky before you start your ride!

Balance and Collection

A horse may be balanced without being collected, but he cannot achieve true collection without being balanced. A horse is said to be balanced when his weight is distributed equally over his hind and front legs. So he may be balanced for jumping with a different outline and longer base than that required for a collected trot à la dressage. This is where once again the half-halt is so important. In collection one requires the horse to carry his neck high and arched with the muzzle in line with or above the withers; hocks flexing to carry the weight which has been put onto the quarters which will

Horses in balance – dressage (LEFT) *and show jumper* (RIGHT)

The upper horse is 'croup high' and may tend to be on the forehand; the lower horse is
likely to be better balanced

(or should) be lowered, with the hip stifle and hocks all doing their part in flexing and carrying. The neck must come up from impulsion (i.e. forward movement) from the quarters and hind end, it must never be put or pulled up from the front only. The essence of collection is the shortening of the base and length of stride *but*, and this is an important but, with increased impulsion through flexion upwards of the hocks and knees, I often say collection is in fact collecting energy!

Collection is obtained over a period of time, little by little, and only collect to the level to which your horse is capable. This is where I like to use the long reins, particularly on a young horse, as I can see what I am doing, and the horse can do his collection without the weight or disturbance of the rider. Collection in the beginning should only be held for a few strides then the horse should relax, thus learning to enjoy his collected work. If he learns good balance, he should learn collection easily so long as he is not over-asked.

Some horses, due to their conformation and possibly their breeding, find collection easier than others. There is no doubt that the German Sport Horse is a powerful animal with exceptional impulsion which can produce and maintain collection for a considerable time. However, a Thoroughbred who is bred to gallop, finds collection more difficult with his lower action and often narrower body, and the inherited wish to gallop which can lead to temperament difficulties in dressage.

6.
THE AIDS

The Aids Explained

The aids are signals by which we tell the horse what to do. They act, resist and yield. The horse should respond 'rightly, lightly and with energy' when an aid is applied.

There are three natural aids – the legs, the hands and the rider's body weight. There is also the voice (not allowed in competitive dressage), but a most important training aid. The artificial aids are: whip, spurs, martingales and various other pieces of equipment, such as running reins and bearing reins. Spurs, although classified as artificial are in fact mandatory in certain dressage competitions and are part of the dress in the show ring.

The application of the aids is divided into two categories – diagonal and lateral. Diagonal aids are used to create forward movement and in collection. They are also in advanced lateral movements such as the half-pass. Lateral aids are applied for the easier lateral movements such as shoulder-in and leg yielding.

In the case of diagonal aids the acting leg aid will be on one side of the horse, whilst the acting hand/rein aid will be on the opposite side, i.e. left and right or vice versa. The acting hand and leg action must be supported by their opposites.

The rider's body weight has considerable effect on the horse, the trunk of the body being by far the heaviest point. Leaning in any direction will cause the horse to adjust his 'position'. The body weight aid should not be confused with the 'seat bone aid' – it is easy to move weight from side to side or backwards and forwards. The seat bones act when the rider is sitting in balance and presses down on a particular seat bone.

Harmony of the Aids

Learning the aids is relatively simple, but putting them into effect is not. What one is trying to achieve is the co-ordination between two living entities. The hands, legs and body of the rider should mould in with the movement of the horse. Riders should develop feel. If it feels right then it usually is right. Sometimes riders are afraid of actually using an aid for fear of upsetting their horse. My view is that there are very few people who are capable of really hurting a horse. Riders should learn to be confident. Riders who ride for recreation often wish to school their own horses. To create confidence and expand knowledge one of the best things to do is to take some lessons with a qualified instructor on a well trained horse: this will give the feel of movements.

In the application of the rider's aids, there is a time lag between the thoughts being sent to the horse's brain, then to the rider's leg which in turn must touch the sensory nerve in the correct place on the horse's sides which in turn tells the horse's brain which then operates the movement (motor nerves). The whole process takes time. If the legs touch too strongly you may get too strong a reaction with a sensitive horse, and if the lower leg is not too close to the horse's sides there will be a time delay. Timing and feel are important. Aids usually have to be applied earlier *not* more strongly.

The rider's hands and fingers should be supple enough to ensure a steady contact with the horse's mouth. The bars of the mouth (on the jaw) are sensitive as is the tongue and the corners of the lips. An uneven contact is painful to the horse and tends eventually to lead to a bad mouth.

Moving one's body too much is unsightly and a disturbance to the horse, equally a stiff, rigid body causes a lack of harmony. The rider's body should be supple without being sloppy, straight without being stiff, absorbing the movement of the horse as he progresses.

Transitions

Transitions are when the horse goes from one movement to another.

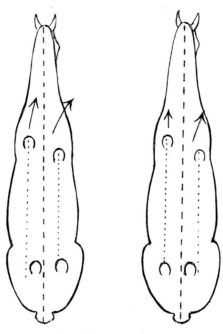

Upward and downward transitions

$\dot{\cap}$ = *Horses's hooves*

They are considered the 'essence' of good training when performed well. When a horse goes from one movement to another he has to adjust himself and carry his rider, so it is crucial that there is as little disturbance as possible. Take for instance going directly from walk to canter, the rider may get dislodged to some extent and cause the horse to move jerkily. Practising transitions is part of training. If you analyse a dressage test you will be surprised at the number of transitions. Take a test of the standard your horse is working at and list the transitions and then practise them.

In a Novice test these will be transitions to and from halt, walk, trot and canter, some of which may be progressive, but none the less should be smooth.

Transitions upwards are usually easier than the downwards ones, particularly from canter because of the speed and pace of the movement.

The Prix St Georges and Grand Prix tests contain transitions of special difficulty. At the Grand Prix used at Olympic and Championship level, the piaffer and passage transitions are worth double the marks to highlight the importance of collection, balance and suppleness of the horse when performing these movements.

Rhythm and the Half-Halt

The terms 'rhythm' and the 'half-halt' are variously described, often causing confusion.

According to the dictionary 'rhythm' describes the consistent length of strides. The quality of a movement which may be regular is that the tempo should be correct too. Tempo describes the speed of the movement, which means that a horse may move regularly but too fast, such as making short hurried steps – or too slowly and lacking impulsion. Cadence also comes into the reckoning when evaluating a movement. Cadence describes the expression of intonation but it is a difficult word to describe. In the context of horses it, combined with tempo, describes the liveliness, fluency and sound of footfall. Rhythm, tempo and cadence combine to give us correct length of strides, speed of strides and lively regular footfalls – all essential when evaluating movements.

The half-halt – quite one of the most important and influential aids – is a direct translation of the French 'demi-arret' and the German 'half-parade' and it literally means half a halt. In fact what one is trying to achieve is a rebalancing of the horse. It is one of the most important correcting movements in equitation. Rebalancing is used in training to bring a horse to attention and into balance. This is usually achieved by asking the horse to bring his balance (weight) more onto his quarters, i.e. to come off his forehand.

It should also be used to prepare a horse for a new (next) movement. Take for instance, walk to halt, or canter to walk. Both of these are downward transitions, one easier than the other. The half-halt is essential to rebalance a horse so as to achieve a smooth transition. In upward transitions too the preparation is done via the half-halt. Correcting a horse whilst moving can be done with the judicious use of the half-halt. Sometimes several half-halts may be needed successively.

Achieving a half-halt

To obtain a half-halt the rider uses the aid to halt, but as the horse is about to halt, he is allowed to move forward, but in a new balance.

The aids are first applied with the seat and legs to create proper impulsion. As you feel the horse take the bit, close the fingers on the reins and raise the hands just enough to raise the horse's head and neck. Then loosen, but do not drop the rein contact. This will allow the horse to move forward in the new balance. The horse should then be in an easier balance with a slightly shorter, more contained outline. The upward action of the reins should be just momentary.

Timing is very important in the application of aids for a half-halt. If the leg aids are too strong the horse may run through your hand, i.e. keep going with no adjustment of weight. The hand/rein aids, if used too strongly or too early, may cause the horse to raise his neck without proper engagement of the hind legs, thus causing the horse to hollow his back. Judicious and clear co-ordination of the aids is therefore vital. One way of understanding the half-halt is to equate it with soldiers marking time. When marking time, their knees go up and down on the spot, not forward. In the case of a horse, his knees and hocks flex up and down.

The Hands and the Reins

It is through the hands that the reins are used. They guide and control the horse. The hands act, resist and yield. They act when turning a horse and are used to influence the movement of the shoulder and foreleg. They resist when asking a horse to slow down, and yield when allowing the horse to go forward or to relax him, when the horse stretches his neck down.

In theory there should never be an occasion for a backward tension on the reins – although if a horse is running away this principle may not be practical!

The reins should be held in separate hands and be kept either side of the horse's neck. The fingers should be closed on the palms with the reins held between the index finger and the third finger with the thumb closing on the index finger. When tightening or closing the fingers on the reins it is the third finger that does most of the work, the remainder of the rein runs between the third and fourth (little) fingers. The wrists bend inwards and are normally situated three to four inches (7.5 to 10 cm) above the pommel of the saddle, and can be held a little higher in very high collection. Reins held too low cause the bit to pull on the base of the horse's mouth. This is not recommended. The hands should be well in front of the ribcage. The gap between the knuckles varies from nearly touching to two to two-and-a-half inches (5 to 6 cm). If the reins are too long and the rider's hands go towards the hips then control is lost.

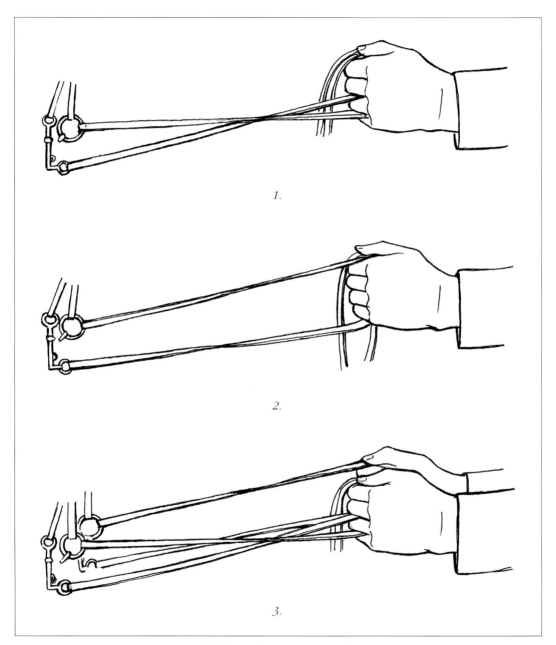

Holding the reins correctly

1. Normal   2. Baucher method   3. Viennese method

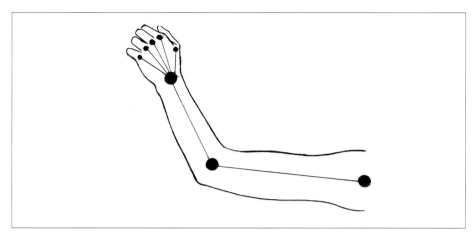

Areas of relaxation in the arm

With the forearm and elbow lying comfortably, the wrists should be flexible and able to open or close as required. The wrist can open three to four inches (7.5 to 10 cm). The arms, wrists and fingers cannot function properly if they are tense or stiff. Contact with the horse's mouth should be constant with a feeling of elastic tension through the reins – not rigid or sloppy, but like a lively tennis ball.

To have an effect on the horse's movement the hands should act (ask) just as the horse's foreleg is about to come off the ground. Not later as this will negate the effect.

The movement of the horse's shoulders, as they move backwards and forwards, makes the following with hands most important. The hands should, as the shoulder comes back, take up the slack on the rein, and go with the forward movement, as the shoulder stretches out, allowing the hands, arms and sometimes the body, to follow the movement.

A good steady contact can be created this way. It may take some time to perfect this 'following' until it becomes automatic. Allowing the horse to move the rider freely at walk will help to create a sense of feel. A helpful exercise is to walk the horse over a pole on the ground and this will exaggerate the horse's movement and help establish the feeling within the rider.

The French *Manual d'Equitation* cites five different reins:

1.   The Direct Rein.
2.   The Opening Rein.
3.   The Indirect Rein in front of the withers.

4. The Indirect Rein behind the withers.
5. The Neck Rein.

The effects of the reins

1 *The Direct Rein*
Used to steady, or stop a horse, also helps in direct flexion. Close
fingers on both reins fairly tightly, but do not pull backwards unless
absolutely necessary.

2 *The Opening Rein*
Used to turn a horse (including pirouette at walk and half-pass). If
turning right, carry both hands to the right, the left one stays near
the left side of the horse's neck, whilst the right hand and forearm
move out towards a position near the rider's right knee. If the horse
is not very well schooled then the hand may have to come out four
or five inches (10 to 12 cm), if he is well schooled then an inch (2.5
cm) will suffice. The rider must remember not to lean or tip over,
only to move the hands and arms.

3 *The Indirect Rein used in front of the withers*
Used to turn a horse round without the help of leg aids, as is the
one used behind the withers. There is however a subtle difference
in that the one used in front of the withers has a very strong effect
on the displacement of the horse's hindquarters to the side, making
the horse, in effect, perform a turn on the centre, front feet and hind
feet each making a circle (or half circle) around the horse's centre
axis. The rider, in using the right rein in front of the withers, keeps
the left hand softly against the horse's neck, and at the same time
slightly back towards the left.

4 *The Indirect Rein used behind the withers*
This rein causes displacement of the horse's quarters, but allows the
forehand to stay put, thus causing a turn on the forehand. The rider
uses the reins in the same way as for No. 3, but brings the hand
back towards the centre button of the riding coat.
    In my opinion this is a most important rein to use and to
understand. It is not difficult to use and most horses will respond to
it straightaway.

5   *The Neck rein*

Used to turn a horse when holding the reins in only one hand. If, for instance, one wishes to turn a horse to the right, and is holding both reins in the left hand – which being the 'bridle' hand is often the case – one should have an even rein contact with the horse's mouth, and at the same time carry the left hand until it and the left rein are touching the left side of the horse's neck. This puts more weight onto the horse's right shoulder and he will, himself, follow this weight displacement.

I will not go into greater detail – if the rider wishes to consult one of the many excellent publications on equitation a much deeper study may be made. Suffice to say that in the application of all aids, kindness and clarity are paramount and the 'acting' rein is the one which does the work, whilst the 'supporting' rein does just that – supports its neighbour.

The German *Official Handbook* cites four ways of using reins:

1.   The Regulating Rein.
2.   The Yielding Rein.
3.   The Supporting Rein.
4.   The Non-Allowing Rein.

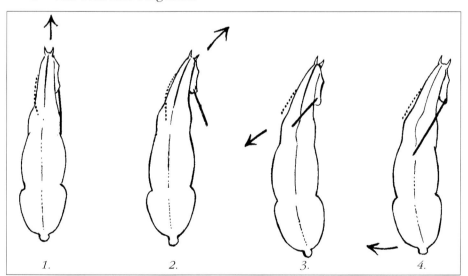

The rein effects

The Regulating Rein is used in conjunction with the rider's weight and leg aids. The horse must be 'on the bit':

a. to make a downward transition
b. to shorten the stride within a pace
c. to halt or rein back
d. to flex the horse
e. to make the horse alert.

The Yielding Rein is used to ask the horse to lengthen his neck.

The Supporting Rein is used to balance and control the inside (lateral) bend of the horse's head and neck. It is only applied by the outside rein.

The Non-Allowing Rein is used to contain the energy created by the seat and leg aids. The rider's hands should yield, momentarily, so that the horse keeps light in hand and does not lean on the rider's hand. Nor should the rider try to place the horse's head with the rein, rather contain the horse between hands and legs.

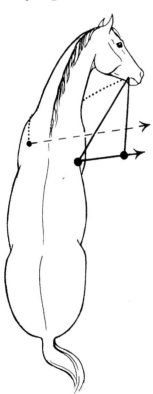

The Opening Rein

The Opening Rein

To show position, action and effect of this rein aid.

1. The continuous line from the horse's mouth to the large dot shows the position of the opening rein to the hand. There are two right hand positions shown, the one nearest the horse's neck is the one of lesser degree of effect (for a fully schooled horse);
    the one furthest from the horse's neck is for a less well schooled horse.
2. The smaller dots indicate the supporting hand.
3. The arrow pointing to the right on the continuous line shows the continued effect of the opening rein.
4. The broken line from the small dot shows the direction in which the horse's weight is displaced thus, with no leg aids, causing the horse to turn his shoulders to the right.

The Indirect Rein (used behind the withers)

To show position, action and effect of this rein aid.
1. The continuous line shows the position of the rein, and the large dot the position of the acting hand.
2. The smaller dots indicate the supporting hand.
3. The broken line from the right shoulder and right hip of the horse shows the effect the rein has, and the direction of the horse will move in, i.e. as this (right) rein is used it will cause a displacement of the horses's body weight to the left, which without the right leg aid, will make the horse's quarters move around his shoulders – thus turning on the forehand.

The Leg Aids

The leg aids, like the hand aids, act, resist and yield. They act when asking the horse to move forward on the turn, they resist when closing the knee and thigh, as in halting. The leg is also used to correct a horse, such as when not standing square in halt, or when placing a leg out of alignment when on a circle. It will be seen that the rider's legs have an

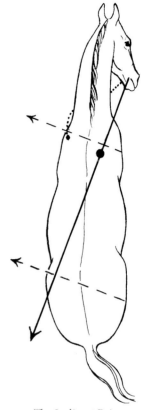

The Indirect Rein

important job to do. The legs yield when lessening the pressure once a horse is in motion, or has obeyed a signal.

One of the first things a young horse must learn is to go forward from a touch of the legs. This is often referred to as accepting the rider's leg. However, the horse must also learn to accept the leg in collection – or in the beginning to accept the leg as the horse accepts the bit, i.e. when the horse learns to arch his neck and relax his jaw. He must also learn to move away from the rider's leg when asked. It is useful to consider the clarity of leg aids. Usually the rider asks for impulsion and submission by applying the inside of the heel of the boot – or the spur if worn, near the girth. For lateral movements or moving away from the leg, a particular spot behind the girth should be used so that there is not confusion in the horse's mind.

For a horse to accept the leg properly in collection much of the power of the aid comes via the rider's thigh and calf muscles, which when the heel is lowered tightens the calf and thigh which squeeze against the saddle and ribs. This is a very powerful aid and riders should learn to lower and then relax the heel and ankle to find the right pressure for the horse concerned.

The rider's legs should be applied just as the hind leg is about to come off the ground. The legs act and support in harmony. Never grip all the time as that will deaden the sensory nerves, and the message will take a long time to get to the brain. This is known as being dead to the leg. Some horses' reaction to leg aids are slower than others. The sensory nerves can be developed by judicious use of the legs.

The Seat Aids

The rider's seat as an aid is very powerful. Seat bones can be used:

a.   With weight equally on both bones.
b.   With weight on one seat bone more then another.

It should be thoroughly understood how to make the best use of the seat bones. The rider's weight must press down onto the seat bones but not all the time. It is essential to develop a light seat. Pressing down heavily all the time will bruise a horse's back and eventually the horse will not bother to respond to the seat bones at all. To take the pressure off the seat bones the rider should channel some of his weight down the front of his thighs and inside of the calves. To bring the weight onto the seat bones the rider should straighten his upper body and adjust his weight from the thighs onto the seat bones, sitting taller but not leaning back with the weight ready for use.

To actually use the seat bones, there are occasions such as when collecting a horse, when a rider's shoulders should come behind the perpendicular but only momentarily. This is to bring the weight onto the seat bones at an angle and is rather like tipping a chair forward with one's seat. This use encourages impulsion and engagement of the hindquarters.

Seat aids, like all aids, should be used in conjunction with leg and rein aids.

Placing more weight on one seat bone than the other or actually moving the pelvis forward on one side, acts as a weight aid for the horse to follow. It is used as an aid to turn, and in a well schooled horse, a slide of the seat and a glance in the direction of movement will be enough signal that the horse needs to make a turn (less well schooled horses will need a hand and

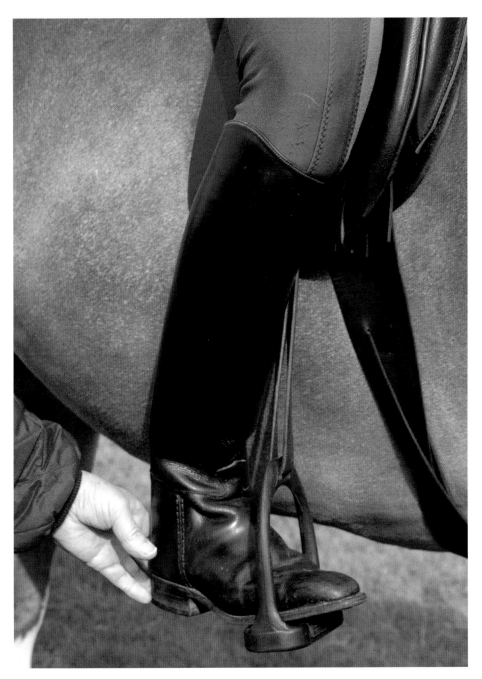

Correct lower leg position (JOHN EVANS)

leg aid of varying degree). The use of the seat bone is useful in lateral work – the horse will follow the weight. To become familiar with which seat bone is which, sit on both, then transfer weight to first one bone then the other bone. The seat bone aid is used extensively for canter strike off. Whether it be lateral or diagonal aids the weight on the correct seat bone is essential.

Contrary Body Movement

This is a phrase with which some people may not be familiar, but it was one of Einar Schmit Jensen's key explanations. It is best described by saying the rider's shoulders should be parallel to the horse's shoulders whilst the rider's hips should be parallel to the horse's hips.

This means that when a horse is going in a straight line the rider should

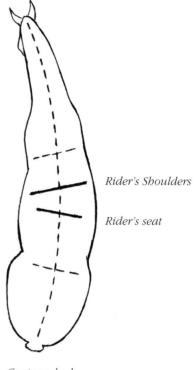

Rider's Shoulders

Rider's seat

Contrary body movement

sit centrally and straight. However, on a curve, turn or circle, whilst keeping the elbows lightly touching the rider's hips, turn the shoulders and hips slightly in the direction of the movement. This will bring more weight onto the inner seat bone. Keeping the elbows lightly touching the rider's hips, this will automatically lengthen (but not stop contact with) the outside rein, and shorten the inside rein and thus the horse will turn automatically.

Obviously this aid is used on horses which are reasonably advanced, and do not need the opening rein. Although the rider's body position can assume the 'contrary' position and at the same time use the inside opening rein with the inside hand. This will enable the horse to learn to circle turn correctly.

The outside of the circle is larger in circumference than the inside, the horse's hips and shoulders are further apart on the outside, and the horse's legs take longer steps whilst the inside hips and shoulders are closer together and the steps shorten, with the hind legs more under the horse's body.

Be careful to maintain an even contact with the reins, never pulling the horse onto his forehand and maintaining the balance with the outside rein.

Analysis of Hand and Leg Uses

An analysis of the use of the hands and of the rider's legs is useful. One of the first things to define is the movements made by the horse's shoulders, neck and head. The other thing is the sequence, and thus the co-ordination of all the legs at the different paces. Obviously, these sequences vary according to the pace – walk, trot, canter or gallop, or rein back.

Sequences

Walk: 1. Left hind. 2. Left fore. 3. Right hind. 4. Right fore.

Trot: 1. Left hind and right fore together. 2. Right hind and left fore together.

Canter: (near) fore leading.
1. Right hind. 2. Left hind and right fore together. 2. Left fore (leading leg) Right (off) fore leading. 1. Left hind.
2. Right hind and left fore together.
3. Right fore (leading leg).

Gallop: Left (near) fore leading.
1. Right hind. 2. Left hind. 3. Right fore. 4. Left fore (leading leg) followed by period of suspension.
Right (off) fore leading. 1. Left hind. 2. Right hind.
1. Left fore. 4. Right fore (leading leg) followed by a period of suspension.

Rein-Back: 1. Left hind and right fore together. 2. Right hind and left fore together.

The rider should learn the sequences and then having memorised them, learn to feel them. At first this will be a question of the rider having to think out what is happening. Later this process should become automatic.

When a horse is walking he moves his head from side to side and his shoulders move forward and back. Even though the rhythm of the walk is four beats it is often easier to pick up a one/two rhythm with the hands following the shoulders. In trot it is said that the horse keeps his head still. This is possible, but in fact the neck does move from side to side. The rider's hands therefore do still need to follow the shoulders. In canter, the beat is three time, so the hands and wrist need to pick up a definite one/two/three feel, scooping up the slack in rhythm with the leading front leg. In the rein back the hands (wrists) follow the movement of the shoulders as the horse takes diagonal steps backwards.

The inside of the rider's legs from the hips downwards are in contact with the saddle and then to approximately one third of the inside calf of the rider's leg with the horse's rib cage. The lower leg drops down into the stirrup, just a fraction away from the ribs. The whole leg should lie comfortably, not gripping, but ready for use. In keeping close to the rib cage the legs should feel the ribs expand and flatten out as the horse moves. They expand as the horse's hind leg comes forward and thus push the rider's leg slightly forwards. The rider's leg should be sensitive enough to feel what is happening.

At walk the rider's legs should be quiet, at trot they should absorb the movement in two time, at canter three time. Both the hands and the legs should act just as either the front or hind legs are *about* to come off the ground, *not* when they are already on the ground.

At all times the rider should remember the adage 'Legs without hands and hands without legs' – not all together.

The Voice

The use of the voice is not allowed in a dressage test. There are many people who will not use it in training, believing the horse will rely on the voice rather than the rider's aids.

Personally, I do use the voice as a training aid in the first instance. I am sure the horses appreciate it, as they do a 'pat' as a reward. When I am training a horse, particularly on the lunge-line, I use my voice, a) as a command to 'walk-on' or 'trot-on' or 'canter' and 'halt', b) as an encouragement to slow down – or go faster. For some reason I really don't know, I often use the French word '*allez*' to mean go, or hurry up and '*douce*' or '*doucement*' to slow down. The tone of the voice and the position and aids applied by the rider, all come into play, so that in the end the horse answers the rider's aids, rather than solely the voice.

When riding, it is reassuring that a horse will (or can) respond to a growl, or a soothing 'whistle', or soft word.

The association of ideas is relevant. Using the voice means something and this is remembered by the horse. For instance to 'walk-on' say this and apply your leg at the same time. Then once the horse is used to the voice, use the legs but not the voice. By then the horse will associate the leg aid with 'walking on'.

When using the voice remember to be clear in your command. Each word should have a slightly different intonation – 'WALK-on', 'TERROT-on', 'CANTer' – or in French 'GaLOPP'.

The author riding the Thoroughbred Lough Thorn and applying a very light seat aid
(FIONA FORBES)

7.
SADDLERY

Whips and Spurs

Whips

Whips and spurs are essential extra 'helps' in horse training but they most certainly should not be used in anger or in such a way as to injure a horse. Whips come in all weights and lengths. A schooling whip should be approximately thirty inches (76 cm) in length and made up of light weight fibre glass of a thickness that has some flexibility – a very soft thin whip does not give the right feel when applied. The handle should be of non slip material and have a knot on the end to stop the whip slipping through the rider's hands. The whip should normally only be applied on the horse's ribs (behind the rider's boot) to indicate forward movement, or to teach a horse to move sideways. A trainer (dismounted) may assist a rider by applying a training or lungeing whip near the hocks to assist bringing them further under him as in piaffer and passage.

Used on the lower shoulder or the front legs this should only be done when asking for the Spanish walk. The whip should on no account be used near the head for fear of injury to the face or eyes. Show jumping riders may encourage a horse to go faster by a smack on the neck, but they should not raise their hands.

Asking for attention or making a punishment by use of the whip must be one short smack to indicate correction, in the case of a punishment this must be immediate to the situation or it is of no value.

Riding with two schooling whips is the proper way to enhance leg aids. With two whips no changing of hands is necessary, the whip can be applied with immediacy and with no disturbance.

Short whips (approximately fifteen inches – 38 cm) are correct for show jumping and cross-country work, or for hacking. They are thicker than a schooling whip, and have a piece of folded leather at the end, which has the added stimulus of making a noise when applied.

Whips may only be carried in certain Novice dressage tests, and must be not more than thirty-two inches (81 cm) in length.

Spurs

Spurs, like whips, should only be used to supplement the rider's leg aid, and never in such a way as to injure a horse. There are many different types of spurs. Normally what is known as 'The Prince of Wales' pattern is used, that is a spur with a slightly downward curve and of about half-an-

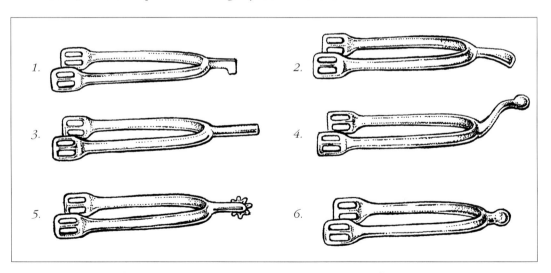

1. Square Block Spur
3. Straight Neck Spur
5. Rowelled Spur

2. Prince of Wales Pattern
4. Swan-Neck Spur
6. Tom Thumb button Spur

inch (12 mm) length. There is a spur of the same length but with a straight neck, and a spur with a square neck which is shorter. For decorative use a 'Tom Thumb' button spur is used. Military spurs are known as 'Swan-necked', that is curved upwards and attached to the heel of the rider's boot as opposed to the 'Counter' (just below the rider's ankle bone). A correctly fitted spur should touch the horse just behind the girth, where the heel would normally touch. Spurs can and should be used clearly but softly, one feather-like touch is all that should be necessary. Riders can learn this action, and learn never to ride with the spurs constantly against the horse's sides. Horses will learn to accept spurs if they are used judiciously. Rowelled spurs should only be used for special purposes. Short spurs are the most suitable for jumping.

Stirrups

The dressage rider uses a stirrup which is weighted at the foot area to ensure that the stirrup leather between the stirrup bar and the stirrup is straight.

Bits and Bitting

There is a saying 'Is the bit a necessary evil?'. So what is the use of a bit? Control is the obvious answer. To obtain control of your horse I use the metaphor 'maximum control with minimum effort'.

Dressage stirrup with weighted foot area (JOHN EVANS)

That effort will depend upon a number of things, such as the pace required, the temperament of the horse and the shape of the horse. It must also include the rider's ability to use properly the bit which is in the horse's mouth.

I am basically a snaffle and double bridle person. However, I do on occasions use certain other bits for a specific reason, and it is always important to 'bit' a horse correctly, i.e. so that he goes easily with 'maximum control with minimum effort'.

Foot correctly positioned in the stirrup (JOHN EVANS)

The size of the bit should be decided by looking at and examining the horse's muzzle and mouth. Some horses have very narrow jaws, some, rather wide ones. The bars of the mouth – that area on the lower jaw where there are no teeth but there is feeling, can be very sharp and narrow, others fat and wide. The effect of the bit lying correctly on the bars will cause no pain, whereas if a very thin snaffle lies directly on sharp narrow bars this will cause discomfort and probably cause the horse to throw his head about.

The horse's tongue is another factor; a large tongue within the horse's mouth clamped shut by a tight noseband will cause the horse to bite his own tongue, a very uncomfortable situation to which the horse will react.

A bit that is too wide will not lie correctly and will cause pressure (and in some cases rubbing) on the muzzle area, and a bit that is too narrow will pinch the muzzle – so it is vitally important that the bit fits. I find that because I ride relatively small horses a four to four-and-a-half inch (10 to 11cm) mouthpiece is usually acceptable.

The action of the snaffle is upwards and nutcracker-like, the action of the curb is downward. This leads to counter action if you are using a double bridle and I use the following sequence with split second timing or feel: a) legs on, b) bridoon action, c) curb action. One can pick up a rhythm by saying to oneself 'legs, bridoon, bit'. 'Bit' being another word for the curb bit. Legs are for impulsion, the bridoon to raise the neck and head of the horse, and the curb is to ask for the flexion of the jaw. Together with sympathetic half-halts this will (or should) lead to more balance and collection. With weight being on the horse's hindquarters, and although his muzzle may be quite high – withers height in passage and piaffer – he should never be over bent.

Now the pattern of controversy and debate creep in – why if one is taught to ride a young horse in a snaffle and keep his neck low and long do I say the snaffle has an upward action?

I was brought up to think of three phases to a horse's training: a) long and low, b) medium balance and c) finally raise the head and neck in conjunction with the hind legs to obtain complete balance and collection. This final phase is quite difficult to arrive at, and rather like backing a young horse, when is the best time to do this? Feel and experience are really the only answer. I think one can arrive at the medium, that is general purpose phase in about a year. For early jumping and cross-country one does not need to go beyond this phase of balance, but to perfect it. For Grand Prix dressage it will take anything up to four years to arrive at a perfect piaffer and full collection.

It is true that the snaffle has an upward effect when used as a bridoon with the curb bit, (i.e. double bridle), and when raising a horse's head, and keeping one's hands rather high. If one carries one's hands rather low but not pulling down, then the action of the snaffle bit comes onto the bars of the mouth as opposed to the lips. A drop noseband not too tight and approximately four inches (10 cm) above the nostrils is useful to encourage a young horse to lower and lengthen his neck. One also needs to adjust one's position in the saddle, i.e. take the weight off the back of the saddle, thus allowing the horse to use his back muscles and even tail, all the way through to his head. Having stretched and built up the muscles along the back and the neck, this will allow the horse to use his quarters and hind legs correctly as well as his shoulders and forelegs. This is a basic principle upon which to build a collection.

Snaffles and Other Bits

Snaffles come in a variety of shapes and sizes. It is often difficult to choose the best one for your horse. The names of the various snaffles are also confusing.

The snaffle most often used on a young horse is the German loose ringed snaffle, which has a thick mouth piece and is jointed. It may be hollow mouthed, in which case it is very light. Some horses will accept this bit with no trouble, but I prefer to have either a fairly tight cavesson (ordinary) noseband, or a properly fitted drop noseband to keep the bit in the correct place in the horse's mouth. This probably applies to nearly all snaffles.

A snaffle can have various types of rings in the side cheeks, also several different types of surfaces. An ordinary cheek snaffle is useful to keep the bit from sliding sideways out of the horse's mouth. A different type of cheek snaffle known as the 'Fulmer' is popular for young dressage horses. This bit must be attached by leather rings to the cheek pieces of the bridle. The effect of this is that the bit is actually suspended in the horse's mouth, therefore does not damage the bars. A drop noseband is also used and must be carefully adjusted so that the link of the bit does not stick into the roof of the horse's mouth. This bit has the added advantage in that it prevents the horse from getting his tongue over the bit. The 'Baucher' snaffle acts in the same way.

A very popular snaffle is the medium thick egg-butt, a nice smooth mouthed snaffle with moulded sides and a flat ring which is fixed. This is a

Bits

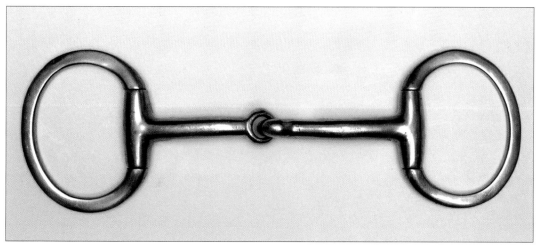

Ordinary egg-butt snaffle (JOHN EVANS)

Thick mouthed egg-butt snaffle (JOHN EVANS)

very useful all round bit. A very thick egg-butt is often too heavy on the bars of the mouth.

Straight and half-moon snaffles are useful on horses which don't like a joint or have a mouth problem. They are usually made of reinforced rubber or vulcanite. A pure rubber mouthed snaffle is not altogether safe, it can snap, and bends when the horse takes hold, and can give a false sense of security.

Roller snaffles are useful for horses which set their jaws, whilst twisted mouth snaffles are very severe on the bars and can cause bruising.

There are numerous versions of snaffles, such as the Scorrier (wire), the Cornish form of twisted. All were invented for horses with mouth problems.

There is the gag snaffle, which has the effect of keeping the horse's head up. Thick mouthed large ringed gags are popular to control horses travelling fast across country. This bit needs a 'stopper' just above the bit ring on the side straps of the bridle headpiece to prevent the bit from running too far upwards and cutting the horse's lip. Gags are available with smooth or roller mouthpieces.

A popular bit for controlling a strong horse or pony is a pelham, although it is not permitted in dressage competitions. The pelham has a single mouthpiece and side cheeks with rings for two reins. It has three actions, upwards, downwards and central. There is a curb chain with this bit, which decides on the severity of the rein action on the bit. People often put a coupling or 'round' on to allow the bit to be used with one rein. Although this has proved a popular way of controlling ponies, it actually goes against the principles of bitting. One should use the reins with a slight time lag in between – top rein, bottom rein, not both together. The top rein acts as a snaffle (upward) action, the bottom rein brings the curb chain into play and this has a downward effect.

Horses like pelhams, they find them comfortable and on a strong horse one does not have to pull against the horse all the time. There are various types of pelham, often invented for 'hacks' in the late nineteenth century. It is important to note that they are not allowed in dressage competitions.

When schooling a horse a good guide as to whether the horse is accepting the bit correctly is to see a little bit of white saliva on his lips (not a great lather). This will show the horse is moving his tongue quietly and thus relaxing his jaw. A horse should champ the bit with a closed mouth. If there is no sign of saliva the horse may well be setting his jaw.

To help create saliva a popular bit is one with a copper mouthpiece. Copper causes gases to form in the mouth, and was first used many

Double linked curb chain used for dressage (JOHN EVANS)

centuries ago. There are bits made with plastic mouthpieces which are very light weight, which are useful.

The bridoon part of a double bridle is usually quite thin and therefore should only be used in conjunction with the curb. It would be over severe on its own and in with curb there is not room for too big a bit.

The Curb Bit

The curb bit is probably the most important bit – it is the classical bit. The ultimate in classical riding is to ride on the curb only on a fully trained horse. So it is a bit that needs understanding – what is its action and how should it be used?

The mouthpiece should lie flat in the horse's mouth, and usually has what is known as a 'port', a small arch in the middle to allow room for the tongue, and for the straight 'canons' (either side of the port) to be used on the bars of the mouth.

The side pieces 'arms' or 'shanks' can be of varying lengths, the longer the upper arms the more pressure comes on the horse's poll. The longer the lower arm the more pressure can be brought to bear on the curb chain. Thus, the longer the 'arms' the more severe the bit. There are two kinds of fixtures of the arms to the mouthpiece, one is solid, the other moveable. The curb chain should lie neatly and comfortably in the curb groove, and the lower arm should make maximum contact with it at a forty-five degree angle. If the arm is nearly horizontal it is not doing anything positive. The contact with the reins should be even and light. In fact there should be no backward tension on the curb rein – no pulling back. The curb should not be used in the classical sense as a brake, but as something the horse balances against with the lightest possible contact. Being a straight bar mouthpiece the rein should be held in such a way that it remains straight in the horse's mouth. There are various ways of holding the reins to achieve this.

Normally one holds the reins in both hands, some people like to have the curb on the outside, some on the inside. The main thing is to know which rein is which. This can be done by having reins of different widths. Personally, I like very thin supple reins, and usually put the bridoon on the thicker rein. In military circles they do the opposite. They also ride with the reins in the left hand only, leaving the right hand free to salute. Officers on ceremonial duties ride off the curb rein, the bridoon rein remaining slack.

The most usual method of holding the reins is for both hands to be used. The bridoon rein comes under the little finger, up the palm and between the first finger and thumb, whilst the curb rein comes up through the third and fourth fingers and joins the bridoon.

A method of holding the reins for classical riding is Baucher's method. Here the bridoon rein comes over the top of the index finger and down the palm. The curb rein comes up the palm and over the index finger, the thumb holding both reins secure.

The movement of the wrists backwards and forwards indicates the amount of pressure required on the bit. This method also means that one virtually cannot use both bits simultaneously.

The method favoured in Vienna is holding the curb reins in the left hand and also the left part of the bridoon rein, with the right hand holding the right part of the bridoon, which can be used to check or direct the horse whilst the curb remains straight in the horse's mouth.

The curb chain mainly used today is the double link metal one. There are also leather curb chains, rubber covered chains and the older single link metal chains. All have their uses. The curb chain should fit so there are no gaps at the sides (sign of too wide a bit), which will cause the chain to rub and press on the narrow jaw bones which protrude under the horse's chin.

In Western riding the horses are often trained in hackamores or bosals (a type of rawhide noseband) and a single curb bit is only introduced when the horse is fully schooled to the weight and seat aids. Remember also that the horse's nose is very sensitive. In Spanish riding the Andalusian horses are often trained with a serratta, a form of metal serrated noseband before the curb bit is introduced.

The Double Bridle

Once a horse is going forward confidently and accepting the snaffle nicely,

Double bridle with thick mouthpiece; the
curb is slightly offset to the left and fixed
(John Evans)

Double bridle with moveable mouthpiece
(John Evans)

then is the time to try a double bridle, consisting of a light snaffle part – the bridoon and a short cheeked curb with a fairly loose curb chain.

If a horse has difficulty accepting a double bridle to begin with then riding him with two snaffles for a few days is often a good introduction.

The bridoon should be a little higher in the mouth than a single snaffle, just wrinkling the corners of the lips. The curb sits just below the bridoon, but not so low that it interferes with the horse's tushes (teeth). The shanks of the curb when brought to a slight angle backwards should bring the curb chain into contact with the under-part of the horses's jaw – the curb groove.

The bridoon should have a soft mouthpiece with almost egg-butt sides. The curb should have a thick mouthpiece with a small 'port' (arch) slightly offset. This is the German type of double bridle. There are many variations – particularly of the curb. Most riders prefer a fixed shank, but for a horse with a 'strong' mouth a movable shank is preferable. Large ports are severe but often stop a horse getting his tongue over the bit.

The rider should think in terms of riding with the bridoon, only using the curb when necessary, with less contact on the curb, but not letting the reins go slack.

How to Fit a Saddle

Saddle fitting is an art. Any saddler worthy of his trade will tell you a numnah is a sign of failure on his part. Not all of us are rich enough to have a saddle for each horse, so resort to a nice fluffy numnah hoping it will compensate for a badly fitting saddle. Horses used in top International competitions, dressage and show jumping, do wear numnahs and this is an extra precaution so that the horse uses his back muscles to the full. It is not to compensate.

A properly fitted saddle should fit the rider as well as the horse. Cavalry saddles of old were designed for long distance riding, with evenly distributed weight over the lumbar muscles. Cavalry horses had to

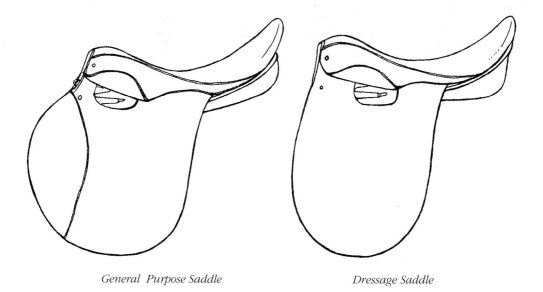

General Purpose Saddle   *Dressage Saddle*

Saddle well positioned on the horse's back (JOHN EVANS)

be sound and unnecessary injuries were not tolerated – the horse had to last. The Cavalry and the Mounted Police use this type of saddle to this day. Our general purpose saddles are derived from the original Army version.

To fit a saddle one should try it on the horse concerned. Take the saddle and place it on or in front of the withers and slide it gently back into the riding position. If it sits there happily and doesn't look like sliding about, then it is in the correct place. If it sits up too high or presses down on the withers then it doesn't fit. You should be able to see a narrow channel of light between the withers and the end of the saddle. The padding either side should be firm and both thick enough and flat enough to carry and distribute the rider's weight evenly. One thing to look out for is whether the front part of the saddle tree or the padding presses on the horse's shoulders or whether the padding is so thin at the back that there is pressure on the back bones. Either is wrong.

If the saddle is secondhand look to see if the padding is worn or the leather or stitching rotten. See if the padding is worn on one side more than the other. 'Sitting crooked' is a favourite remark with dressage judges. Uneven padding is often caused by a rider always riding the same diagonal when trotting.

The weight of a saddle is important. Saddle trees used to be made of beechwood and were solid. Then the Spring tree was introduced with a flexible piece of metal inserted. Later still fibre glass was introduced and is used extensively today, twelve to fourteen pounds is a nice weight for a saddle. Perhaps a bit more for a gentleman's hunting saddle.

Saddles are measured from front to back (pommel to cantle). The usual length for a lady's saddle is seventeen-and-a-half inches (43 cm) and a gentleman's eighteen inches (45 cm). This is average, smaller people and larger ones will require shorter or longer. Saddle trees come in three widths, narrow, general purpose (medium) and wide.

A saddle should have a good wide comfortable seat to allow the rider to sit comfortably. A saddle with a high cantle and knee and thigh rolls tends to restrict a rider's flexibility in the saddle, causing constriction and stiffening. A rider should not have to be held in place by the saddle. Covered foam rubber on the saddle flaps is pleasant for cross-country or for show jumping. In a dressage saddle, the stirrup attachment is set further back than on a cross-country or show jumping one, because the horse's balance is further back.

High quality pig skin is the best for the seat and flaps, the linings may be of leather (easy to keep), linen (can be washed and looks nice), or serge (not so easy to keep, but holds its position on the horse's back well).

Where to Sit in the Saddle

One of the most important things to learn when trying to school a horse successfully is to achieve an independent secure seat. Rein aids, leg aids and the whole balance of horse and rider depend on it. Therefore a correctly fitted saddle is essential. The rider should sit (and fit) easily into the seat, preferably into the narrowest part (waist) of the saddle, with three or four inches (7.6 to 10 cm) of cantle showing and one or three inches (2.5 or 7.6 cm) of pommel; the rider's seat can come to the outside edges but allowing the padding and sides to distribute the weight and support the saddle seat.

A young horse say aged three to five years will usually need a general purpose saddle to allow the weight and balance to remain central. Once you have decided on the horse's speciality – jumping or dressage, then you may need to obtain a specialist saddle.

To achieve an independent seat the rider's legs should be close to the horse's sides. The insides of the thighs staying flat against the leather, whilst the calf should be close to the horse's ribs. Although one is supposed to keep a straight line from the back of one's head to the heel of one's boot sometimes it is necessary to keep the heel a little further back (allowing a spectator to see the girth) but not so far back as to lose balance. Riding without stirrups is helpful in bringing the rider's seat bones into place and thus allowing the legs to lengthen and cover as much of the horse as possible. The rider's balance should be centred over a point just behind the horse's withers and about half way down the horse's ribs. This must and will allow for the flexibility of the rider's thighs and lower leg. Secure without being stiff is the criteria. Riding bareback is another way of achieving this – start at the halt and walk on a quiet horse. If the rider is secure in the saddle then the rein aids can be used as required.

When schooling a young horse (or indeed any horse), it is important to have a saddle that does not interfere with the movement of the horse's muscles situated under the saddle, either side of the spine. Young Thoroughbreds have thin muscles here and these need developing, whereas a Continental Warmblood has stronger, thicker muscles and can perform collected movements earlier.

Cantering is a pace whereby the speed and thrust of the horse can cause loss of balance by the rider. It is better to start canter work with the weight firmly in the stirrup and the seat bones just off the saddle. Once the horse is happy in the movement then if training for dressage one may start to ease the weight into the saddle allowing the horse to carry the rider comfortably. It may take a week or two for the horse to become relaxed.

Always remember that saddle fitting and the correct use of a saddle is for the comfort of horse and rider and to enable the rider to use the aids properly.

8.
SCHOOLING

Straightening

To 'straighten' the horse needs special analysis, regarding the horse's natural curvature. It has little to do with a horse which is 'one-sided' in its mouth. No horse is born entirely straight through his spine. One of the aims of schooling is to develop the horse's muscles so that the horse becomes straighter.

In ninety per cent of horses the natural curvature is to the left, approximately ten per cent of horses have natural curvature to the right. The muscles on the left side of the neck are over developed and hard and the horse does not flex his jaw so easily on the left side. The muscles on the right side are less developed and the jaw is softer and flexes more easily. The right hand side is often referred to as the soft side. The hind legs are in different positions as well. The right hind leg is positioned out to the right, and the left one is usually in line with the left front leg. The right hind leg sends impulsion towards the left front leg and shoulder.

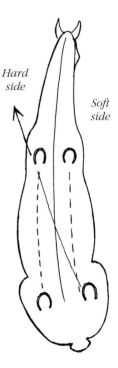

Hard side

Soft side

Natural curvature

And although this can hardly be seen from the ground, it can be felt.

One of the best ways to encourage straightening is to work the horse on the long side of the arena, on the right rein, bringing the horse's forehand slightly off the track to the inside. This brings more weight onto the horse's right shoulder and puts the right hind leg into position with the quarters. The hind legs come a little closer together. When the horse does a proper shoulder-in on the right rein this will work on the left neck muscles and help soften them. Once the horse starts to use his right shoulder freely this will help in obtaining 'lightness' of the forehand and eliminate uneven steps in trot, both in front and behind. Horses who show unevenness in the trot are often 'muscle bound', because of the natural curvature. Unevenness manifests itself by the horse appearing to have hard, tense back muscles. If a horse is particularly stiff, especially on circles, it is a good idea to make two circles, on the bad rein to every one on the good rein.

Circles, Turns and Corners

Circles

The riding of turns and circles is both basic and important in the schooling of any horse. Often how to ride them is not understood.

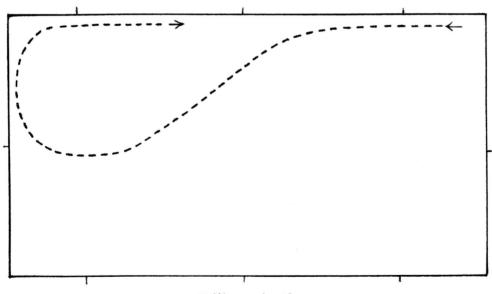

Half loop to the side

A circle is one of the first movements taught to a young horse. The first thing is for the rider to adjust weight onto the leading (or inside) seat bone. This will encourage the horse to follow the weight. The inside rein gives the flexion to the inside, the inside leg creates the impulsion whilst the outside leg controls the quarters. The horse's hind feet should follow on the touch of the front feet at all times.

The size of the circle should be in keeping with the suppleness – the ability to flex the joint laterally without causing the horse to deviate the quarters out of the circle – or having a 'wrong bend' with head and neck. To start with a circle should be large – say fifteen to twenty metres. Gradually, it can be reduced to ten to fifteen metres. If it is smaller than that it becomes a volte (eight metres). Introduce circles at walk and then graduate to trot – working to start with, later medium or collected.

Serpentines

This is a movement used in all Novice and Preliminary dresssage tests. It consists of three half circles as illustrated in the diagram.

Turns

A balanced turn is a sign

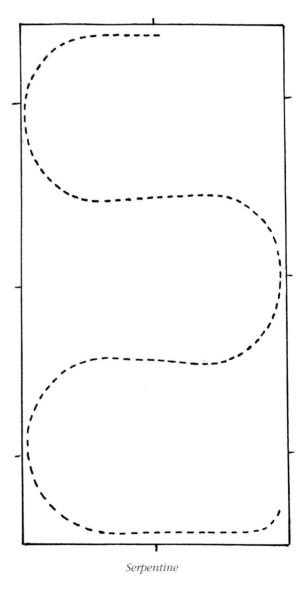

Serpentine

of a horse's ability to collect and carry himself. To turn a horse in motion diagonal aids are used. A turn is actually part of a pirouette. There are three turns from the halt (1) pirouette at walk, (2) turn on the forehand, and (3) turn on the centre.

Making a turn at right angles – walk the horse in a straight line, prepare by use of the half-halt, keep him gathered and balanced. The rider should turn his head and shoulders in the direction of the turn. Keep the inside leg close to the girth for impulsion and the outside one on the ribs to control the quarters. The rider's weight is on the seat bone in the direction of movement, the hand asking for the flexion is the one on that side (inside). Often a turn of the rider's head and shoulders will suffice on a well trained horse. Give a little with the outside rein to allow movement of neck and to maintain balance.

With a young horse or a horse very much on the forehand, it may be a good idea to keep the horse's neck straight and not to overflex to the inside. Keeping contact with the outside rein means the horse's weight must go onto his quarters. Too much inside flexion will result into much weight going into the horse's forehand.

Corners

A corner should be treated as part of a circle. The tightness of the corner should be commensurate with circles of ten to fifteen or twenty metres, the horse's hind feet following in the track of the fore feet all the way and with the correct lateral bend.

Both for dressage purposes and ordinary purposes the corner should be regarded with respect. When approaching a corner the horse may try to slow up particularly if he sees the wall of the arena directly in front of him. Also because of the diversion off a straight line the horse automatically (if allowed) takes a short stride with his inside limbs. This causes both loss of impulsion and balance. The horse will come out of the corner dis-organised.

Approaching a corner (in a riding arena) eighteen to twenty feet (5.5 to 6m) before it, half-halt the horse to bring him to attention and to increase the impulsion. With a lazy horse it may be necessary to increase pace as you approach a corner. The horse should learn to engage his hind legs properly and to balance, thus coming out of the corner ready to obey the rider's next command. On coming out of the second corner it is quite a good idea to lengthen the horse's stride either straight down the long side, or across the diagonal of the school (quarter marker via x to quarter marker). This will encourage impulsion. Obviously with a free going horse this is not necessary. When show jumping particularly indoors, it is important to use the corner well so as to approach the next jump correctly. Course builders like to test a rider by placing a jump close to a corner.

The author's Oldenburg stallion Adel being ridden by his previous owner Frau Schaeffer at Weisbaden (ABOVE) showing good balance and extension and (BELOW) a working-in photograph in a semi-collected canter (this was before the days of the hard hat ruling)

9.
MOVEMENTS

The Halt and the Rein-Back

The Halt

Standing still and halting to attention are two very different things. Immobility is part of halting. When a horse is young, he should be taught to stand still by the rider stopping to have a chat with a friend when out hacking. This probably means that the rider is concentrated on talking and the horse therefore relaxes and is happy to stand (this does not mean forgetting a young horse may move off rather suddenly). This method will however eliminate pulling the horse about and causing a bad reaction.

To halt to attention the rider should at first have the horse in a suitable position in the arena on either the long side or short side, i.e. straight. Put the horse into an organised walk, not too fast, apply one or even two or three half-halts, then apply the stop (halt) aids. Close legs and fingers and straighten your back. Keep the horse there for a few seconds and walk or still 'collected' and then relax. Keep your seat bones central – this is important in respect of the rein-back. Some horses do not stand square until taught to. Front legs under the shoulders too far means the horse is on the forehand and needs more balancing (half-halting) coming into the halt. Hind legs out behind also indicates a lack of preparation for the movement. If a horse persistently leaves one hind leg behind him teach him to respond to a tap from your heel on the side on which he is disobeying. A touch of the heel should tell the horse to move that leg forward. In fact the horse should be taught to bring up either hind leg on command. If the horse is very persistent in this fault then an assistant on the ground can encourage the horse by touching and showing the long whip near the horse's hocks or fetlocks, but do not frighten the horse.

Rein-back

The rein-back is closely related to the halt. It is not always introduced until the horse is quite well on in his training because the horse may use the rein-back as a resistance. Bring the horse to a correct halt, sitting centrally, ask the horse with your hands and legs to go forward and as he thinks of doing so, relax your leg aids and ease your weight very slightly forward. This allows freedom on the horse's back and quarters, whilst still maintaining balance and he can then walk backwards, in diagonals (two time). To go forward again straighten your body and apply the leg aids, whilst lightening but not dropping your rein aids.

It will be seen that the halt, the rein-back and the transition to walk (and later to trot and canter) are interlinked and should be co-ordinated. Horses can walk, trot and canter backwards, although the canter is very difficult and hard for a horse to achieve. Once a horse has learned a highly collected trot this can be translated really easily into trotting backwards and is similar to a piaffer in reverse.

If a horse has difficulty with the rein-back in the beginning, a method of helping this is to practise quarter turns on the forehand to soften the horse's loin muscles. Also when halted ask for a slight lateral flexion as you commence the rein-back. This unlocks the neck and back muscles and makes the rein-back easier. Usually ask for the flexion on the horse's soft (right) side.

When asking a horse to flex at halt (this can also be done when moving), teach the horse to relax his jaw and round his neck by closing your thigh and knees on the saddle just before closing your fingers on the reins. Do not pull your horse's head in or down with your reins, the effect you should feel when you close your legs is that of a tennis ball returning from a practice shot against a wall – with some bounce in it.

The rein-back as required in Olympic tests is often done in conjunction with a set number of steps back and forwards. The important criteria here is to start the rein-back with the correct diagonal and this allows the horse to go forward without difficulty. If proceeding for instance straight into a canter on a named leg the horse should automatically be in a position to strike off correctly. With four steps back and straight into canter with the off-fore, the correct diagonal to start the rein-back is the right front leg and left hind leg diagonal. When the horse proceeds into trot this is easy as the trot is a diagonal movement, whereas walk and canter are not. The horse has to break sequence for these two paces.

The Walk

The walk is a pace of four beats, and with a speed of four to six miles per hour for the ordinary walk one can gauge how long it will take to ride a horse from one place to another by averaging about five miles to each hour, using walk and trot. When using interval training the speed of the walk, trot or canter is measured against the distance covered (i.e. four to six, eight to ten, ten to twelve miles per hour).

There are five versions of walk – ordinary, medium, collected, extended, and free walk. In assessing a walk one looks for the quality, that is the activity and the definite four beats, 1.2.3.4. The horse should use his hind legs to provide impulsion together with the shoulders moving freely forward, the horse's head and neck being carried in a comfortable outline. In the collected walk the horse should show a correct centre of gravity and be accepting the bit properly. The front and hind legs take shorter, higher steps as if marking time, the knees bending noticeably and also the hocks. This enables the horse's legs to make carrying effects rather than propelling ones. A horse who in collection pushes too far with his hind legs will put too much weight onto his forehand. This applies to all the paces. The energy collected must stay within the horse ready for use in extensions and for such highly collected movements as piaffer and passage.

The walk is an extremely important pace, not easy to ride correctly. The ordinary walk is the introductory pace for a variety of movements. The medium and extended walks are to show the impulsion together with the stretching of the back, quarter and shoulder muscles. The neck must be lengthened in co-ordination with the rest of the body. Watching the horse's hind feet to see how far they over step the front ones is a good guide. At all walks except the free walk the contact must be kept. The free walk is a pace of complete relaxation.

A fault quite often seen in walking is 'ambling', i.e. walking in laterals. A good way to help overcome this is to slow the walk, or to walk the horse over cavaletti at about 3ft 6 inches (1.06 m) apart. The cause, unless hereditary as in the Paso Fino, is a stiff or damaged back.

The Trot

The trot is a pace of two beats performed in diagonals, i.e. left hind and right fore, and vice versa, The speed of the ordinary or working trot is six to eight miles per hour. The speed and amount of ground covered will depend to some extent on the natural length of the stride of the horse. Some of the carriage breeds are bred to trot long and fast.

There are four recognised types of trot – the working, medium, extended and collected. The trot is the pace at which a horse is worked. It is considered that the most development of muscles and impulsion can be gained at this pace. The quality of the trot is assessed by its regularity and its elasticity and impulsion. As in walk (and canter), the whole should work, each end, and the back. One of the ways to see if a horse is working throughout his whole body is to watch the area behind the saddle, if these muscles are soft and moving then the horse has a 'swing' to his back, which he doesn't have when it is set and stiff. When riding this can be felt when you go to do a sitting trot. A hard stiff back will jolt one about, whereas a soft back will be comfortable.

The working trot is used to encourage a young or stiff horse to carry himself and his rider comfortably and regularly in a good outline. The medium trot is used to create a longer but balanced stride with impulsion. The extended trot is an advanced movement whereby the horse shows extravagant lengthening whilst maintaining a high level of balance. The head and neck must be allowed to lengthen somewhat to allow the front legs and shoulders to give maximum lengthening, to carry the impulsion forward that is created by the hind legs. The collected trot should always be performed 'sitting' so is only introduced at a certain level of training. The carrying effect of the hind and forelegs is a criterion. The flexibility of the pasterns as well as the hocks and knees will be noticeable, however the rider must not slow the horse down too much, as it is the energy that is being 'collected', i.e. impulsion. The horse's head and neck will be higher and more arched, but the horse must never be over bent, i.e the muzzle behind the vertical. The rider should learn which diagonal is which!

A horse should become supple enough for the rider to rise with the

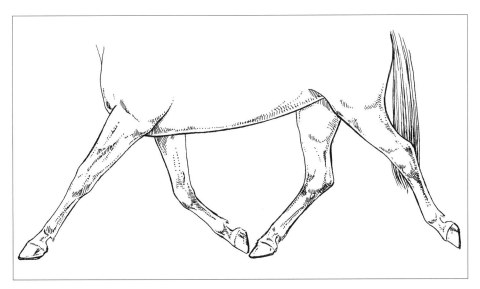

Correct leg movement at trot

diagonal of their choice, rising with either the inside or outside diagonal pair of legs. Changing diagonal can be done either at centre or at the completion of a movement from quarter marker to quarter marker, i.e. just before the second quarter marker. Often in a test this will cause less disturbance. Change the diagonal as smoothly as possible and be consistent in a test so that you keep a particular set of diagonals, i.e. it is usual when going left to ride on the right diagonal, and vice versa. The rider should sit in the saddle as the hind leg is about to touch the ground, i.e. sitting with the right hind and left fore leg, when you are on the right rein means you are riding on the left diagonal because the name is taken from the front leg. The function is to cause the inside leg to engage correctly. When changing diagonals sit for half-a-stride, or if you prefer stay up in the saddle for half-a-stride. A good way to make a transition from trot to walk is to keep the horse well balanced in rising trot and to sit on the last two strides before walk, this will engage the horse's inside hind leg and will help to make a smooth, balanced transition.

A rider should, in rising to the trot, allow the horse to dictate when to rise, being behind or in front of the movement means a lack of synchronisation in applying leg and hand aids, and usually happens when a rider loses balance and is stiff in the upper body. Rising and sitting to the trot should be so smooth that one hardly knows which is which. Rising with

Beatrice Ferrar Salat on Beauvalais shows excellent balance and co-ordination in extended trot in Grand Prix dressage (KIT HOUGHTON)

the movement, which allows the thrust of the horse to be absorbed smoothly by the rider is the criterion. The rider should take the weight onto the front of the thighs and through the knees, which should move ever so slightly as the rider rises. The knees and heels both go down slightly at this moment. Keep the weight in the same place, front of the thighs and down through the knees and heels when performing sitting trot.

To ask a horse to increase the length of stride at trot, in the initial stages rising a little higher will allow the horse freedom to arch his back, and allow the hind feet to come well under the horse. Coming out of a circle, corner of the arena, or just using a stride of shoulder-in will bring the hind legs up, and with a little collection, should help create impulsion and lengthening.

These exercises may also help to lighten a horse's forehand and free his shoulders, as will work over a cavalletti at 4 feet 6 inches (1.37m) apart, increasing to 4 feet 8, 9, or 10 inches (1.42m, 1.45m, 1.47m). Irregularity of strides and moving in laterals are a major fault in the trot, caused either by lack of schooling, loss of balance or a physical defect. The trot should not be ridden at break-neck speed as this leads to all sorts of problems.

The Extended Trot

To achieve a good extended trot the horse should first have and be established in a good working trot, to build rhythm and balance, going on into lengthened strides. Later the horse will graduate to medium trot before attempting the Grand Prix style extended trot, the latter really emanating from balance and collection as well as suppleness.

Some horses of Thoroughbred breeding have a natural tendency to extend and so do some of the German breeds which were originally carriage horses bred for trotting and now amalgamated in Warmbloods.

In either collection or extension the horse should use his quarters and hind legs correctly – that is for collection the hind legs *carry* whereas in extension they *push*. To allow extension of the shoulders and front legs they must have the freedom to actually go forwards. It is a fact that a horse cannot put his foot (hoof) on the ground in front of his muzzle.

The extension of the hind limbs backwards is just as important as the front ones extending forward *with* the horse's shoulders so that the whole horse is extending. If a horse is overbent his weight is on his forehand and he may throw his leg forward only for it to come back to the ground behind his muzzle.

Many horses look 'flashy' by pointing their toes but not using their shoulders. This is incorrect. This type of horse needs re-balancing and learning to loosen his back. Working over a pole or several poles on the ground just at walk often helps to loosen the back and the shoulders. It also helps a novice rider to feel the horse's back moving.

The Canter

The canter is a pace of three beats. These can be counted by the rider – 1.2.3. – quite distinctly. The footfall is: for canter left (cantering with the near-fore leading). 1. right hind, 2. left hind and right foreleg together, 3. left fore (the leading leg). The very slight period of suspension, which is the

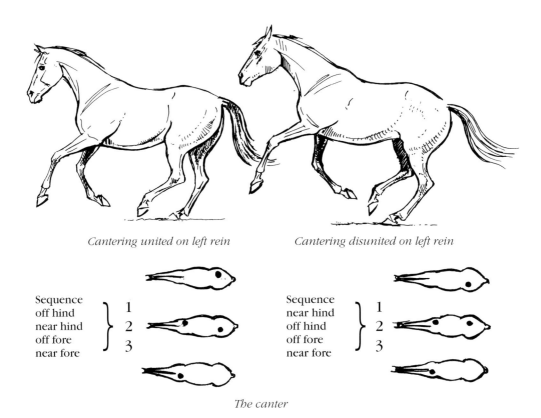

Cantering united on left rein   *Cantering disunited on left rein*

Sequence
off hind   } 1
near hind   2
off fore   3
near fore

Sequence
near hind   } 1
off hind   2
off fore   3
near fore

The canter

fourth point of the canter, is when all the horse's feet are on the ground just as the horse moves his weight from the front leg to the hind one to start the next stride.

In cantering right (cantering with the off-fore leading), the footfall is: 1. left hind, 2. right hind and left fore together, 3. right fore (the leading leg).

There are four types of canter: working, medium, collected, extended, and then the gallop. The speed of the working canter is ten to twelve miles per hour. The canter is different to the gallop both in sequence and speed. Racehorses for instance can attain speeds of forty to fifty miles per hour. Normally young horses are expected to canter from the trot. In the beginning this transition is usually obtained through speed and the loss of balance – this is known as 'falling' into canter. Once a horse has learned to carry his rider quietly in a canter, then it is time to improve the 'strike-off', that is to ask for canter without increasing speed too much and with less loss of balance. The unbalanced horse will try and keep his balance,

Leslie Law riding Shear L'Eau demonstrates correct stretching of the hind legs and foreleg in canter. Note the excellent bending of the neck and body and the rider's soft use of the inside rein (KIT HOUGHTON)

especially on corners by turning his head outwards, giving what is known as a 'wrong bend'. The first lesson in correcting balance should be from a large corner or point of a circle, and to then go straight. It is easier to develop the balance more on the straight line at first.

During the transition for strike-off either from trot or walk there is a split second before strike-off when the horse adjusts his stride. At first this adjustment may be quite lengthy while the horse sorts himself out. Later when he is accustomed to striking-off the adjustment will be hardly noticeable. Because of the speed involved and the power thrust of a horse going into canter, care should be taken to time aids distinctly.

Much has been written about horses' backs. The area from the withers to the croup is vulnerable to injury. Due to the structure of the horse's back, it is not easy to mend any damage. The back connects the front and hind ends and is not actually meant for sitting on, but man has managed to domesticate the horse by sitting on him. It is therefore a good idea to find the place on the horse's back where he can carry the rider most easily. Usually this is just behind the withers, behind the cervical and thoracic muscles. The dorsal muscles under the 'saddle' area are long and thin and do not have much flexibility, the vertebrae (the thoracic and lumbar) are often close together at their tips and damage often occurs in this area, particularly with a long saddle or too much of the rider's weight.

A saddle which is placed on top of the withers area can easily damage the medica nerves which are situated at the bottom of the shoulder blade.

A horse can break the sequence and lead with one leg in front and a different one behind. This is known as being 'dis-united'. The dressage term 'Counter Canter' means that if a horse is moving round the arena to the right he will lead with the outside (left) leg and vice versa. This is a movement used to test the obedience and suppleness of the horse. When teaching it try the serpentine or loops three metres off the straight line or 'wrong' lead at working canter. When working a horse to improve his suppleness it is important to work the horse on both reins, and in both trot and canter. The muscles most used in trot are different to those used in canter. If a horse is stiff in trot some work at canter may help to loosen up the trot muscles.

Working a horse on a long rein in canter is a pleasant reward for the horse and it also helps to calm a horse and to develop a sense of self-balance. Relax the reins gradually until the horse is able to really stretch his neck right out.

The collected canter is the pace used for the pirouette at canter and the flying change *à tempi*. Sometimes one single change is asked for at working or extended canter to test the horse's impulsion and straightness when changing.

The Aids for the Canter

The canter is probably the most confusing of the paces. It causes controversy as to which aid is the best. The aids for the canter are described variously. In the British Pony Club *Manual of Horsemanship* the aid described is diagonal; whilst the German Manual describes an inside lateral aid, and General Decarpentry (France) describe the canter-strike off aid as an outside lateral aid for a horse learning to strike off. All these aids work, timing is the most important thing.

There are in fact three ways of asking for canter.
1)   Outside lateral aids
2)   Diagonal aids
3)   Inside lateral aids.

The outside lateral aid (outside leg and outside rein one of the acting aids) causes the horse to displace his weight to the outside, thus freeing the inside hind, and more importantly, the inside shoulder. Once the inside shoulder is free of weight it can go forwards, and lead.

The diagonal aid is similar to the outside lateral, except that the horse (presumably more balanced by now) carries his head and neck straighter.

The inside lateral aid is the most sophisticated canter aid, to be used on horses which are well balanced and supple. The rider keeps his own weight central, whereas in outside lateral the rider's weight is to the outside (in diagonal aid it is only very slightly to the outside). The rider keeps his outside leg in the supporting role, and as he feels the horse ready (collected and gathered) asks with his inside leg for the actual strike off. Once a horse has learned this, a touch of the rider's inside leg or heel will suffice.

According to General Decarpentry, if the horse is proceeding from walk to canter the leg aid must precede the hand aid, whereas from trot to canter the hand aids must precede the leg aids. These aids are for horses which have progressed from 'falling' into canter in a very unbalanced way.

Again according to General Decarpentry, the horse proceeds into canter from trot by using a front foot first (i.e. right fore for right (off) strike off), whereas from walk to canter right (off) the horse will always start by activating the right hind leg.

The Rider's Position at Canter

As stated in chapter 7 on 'Where to sit in the saddle', I have referred to the canter. Due to the speed and balance of the horse in the various different canters, special attention should be paid to the rider's position on the horse.

Now I need to expand on this. It is my belief that any horse needs basic training. There is a difference of conformation between Thoroughbred and Warmblood in that their back ligaments are different shapes. The Thoroughbred has long thin ligaments whereas the Warmblood has short thick ones; Thoroughbreds are therefore weaker in their backs, particularly when young. With the stronger backed Warmbloods more weight and pressure can be used much earlier than on a Thoroughbred.

To allow the Thoroughbred to, a) use his hind legs with power and b) to allow his back ligaments to develop, it is essential that the rider keeps his/her weight off the back of the saddle, with the weight down through the knees and into the heels. The rider will need to have a shorter stirrup leather and a saddle suitable for general purpose riding.

Both types of horse need to gain and develop balance through using their heads and necks (i.e. with a long neck). Through judicious use of the half-halt over a period of time (six months to a year) the horse's neck will come up and the rider can start to sit deeper and gradually change to a dressage saddle.

The Counter Canter

This is a movement in which the horse canters on the so-called 'wrong' leg. So if travelling on the right rein, the horse will lead with his left foreleg and vice versa. It should only be introduced when the horse is completely obedient to the canter aids and strikes off willingly on either lead. The horse should also be reasonably well balanced in his canter work, going easily on twelve to fifteen metre circles. In other words it is quite an advanced movement.

There are various preparatory movements used to introduce the counter canter. You can make a shallow loop on the straight side of the arena (about three metres) staying on the same lead, or, strike off on the straight side of the school on the outside lead and continue round the corner, which should be made as easy a corner as possible to start with. This is a difficult preparation and really only suitable for a horse ready for collected canter. The easiest way is to ride a twenty metre circle on inside lead, then walk or trot a few paces and strike off on the outside lead, keeping the horse's neck straight so as not to overload the leading (outside) shoulder. Continue for about a quarter of the circle, stop and reward your horse. Continue doing this over a period of weeks until the horse can do the whole circle without difficulty. I like to establish the counter canter completely before trying the flying change.

The Flying Change

The flying change is quite different to the simple change, whereby the horse comes from canter to walk or trot and immediately picks up the canter again with a new leading leg. The simple change is required in dressage tests of Novice/ Elementary Level, and is a basic manoeuvre in any well-schooled horse.

The change of leg at the canter is in fact striking off from the canter into canter. Horses perform it when loose, and do so very smoothly by changing their weight from one side to the other. That is how it is achieved in the polo field. However, in the dressage arena, the judge will look for the

Flying change

complete unity of a collected horse in collected canter. Straightness, engagement of the hind legs and suppleness are taken into account. The first thing to do apart from developing the collection is to make sure the horse is established and completely obedient to the canter aids and will not break when in counter canter. There are several ways of obtaining the change. Cantering in counter canter to the right on a twenty metre circle one can slow right down at a particular point and apply the 'new' canter aid so that the horse actually wants to change. Do not mind the first time how the horse changes, reward him, do it again, once, reward him and leave it until next day. The horse will remember.

Having perfected one change at a time do not hurry the tempi changes, but try a second change say some ten or fifteen paces after the first one and once these are established decrease the distance between changes. Establish the change on one rein before proceeding to the second leg, do the same as for the first but on the other rein.

Another way to introduce the change of lead is to make a half-pass in canter from the centre line of the arena back to the wall (quarter marker) and ask for the change as the horse comes to the corner. The half-pass helps engage the hind legs properly. In any change of leg remember the aid is canter to canter, so reverse the aids. In changes of one time the aids must be applied almost simultaneously. The rider must keep the lower leg close to the horse's sides so as to synchronise their use. The timing is fast and it is easy to get out of rhythm. Once a horse is used to his two time and one time changes he will probably do them almost automatically, so don't over ride in these movements. Smoothness and co-ordination between horse and rider is essential. Impulsion should be created before the movement, maintained as far as possible and then recreated in the next movement.

The Counter Change of Hand

The counter change of hand at canter with flying changes is asked for in Advanced International Competition. It is easier to perform than it looks. In the half-passes left and right the strides are counted in such a way that the horse is ready to change at the right place. So from a six stride one way means the horse is at the point where he can easily change to the new half-pass. The rider applies the aid and gives the new direction, but in fact the horse will not need to change his neck direction too much as this will unbalance him. A touch of the rider's leg will often suffice. Riding a well-balanced horse with a nice 'light' front is quite easy. The pace should be a collected canter with plenty of impulsion. Often just a movement of the reins (side to side) will suffice with no leg aids.

The Pirouette

The pirouette at a canter as required in a dressage test like the other collected canter movements, is quite complex. An about turn is what is required in polo, but the dressage pirouette requires balance, collection and as far as possible the three beats – four beat or fixing of the hind legs are faults. When teaching a horse, the pirouette trainers have their favourite methods, which vary. One of the easiest ways to introduce this movement is via walk pirouette. Half pirouette in collected walk, pick up the pirouette asking for the second part at canter. The walk will have gathered and collected the horse in preparation for the canter.

The Lateral Work I

Lateral work is often thought to consist of shoulder-in and half-pass, but in fact involves a number of movements. In order of difficulty I list the following:

1. Lateral flexions of the jaw: Right or left at halt and walk.

2. Turn on the forehand: Right or left, quarter, half or full turn. Horse's hindquarters circle round the forehand.

3. a) Shoulder-out, b) Shoulder-in: At walk or trot.
   b) Horse's head to the wall, tail at angle of forty-five degrees into the arena, jaw flexed away from direction of movement, and body on three tracks.
   c) Horse's tail to the wall, head at an angle of forty-five degrees.

4. Leg yielding: Horse proceeds on two tracks diagonally across the arena, with jaw flexed away from direction of movement, at walk or trot.

5. Travers: Performed along the wall. The horse faces the wall at an angle of forty-five degrees and proceeds on two tracks with jaw flexed in the direction of movement, at walk or trot.

Sylvia Stanier on the Thoroughbred Lough Thorn being ridden in an American bosal showing a correct lengthened trot. The rider's seat is light and her hands are allowing the horse to stretch his neck (FIONA FORBES)

6. Half-pass: Horse proceeds on two tracks either along the wall, diagonally across the arena, on a circle, or up the centre line. The jaw is flexed in the direction of movement at walk, trot or canter.

7. Counter change of hand: Transition from half-pass to half-pass. At walk, trot or canter.

8. Pirouette: Right or left, quarter, half or full turn, at walk, canter or piaffer. Horse's forehand performs a circle around the hindquarters (can be introduced at walk after turn on forehand).

9. Full pass: Horse proceeds right or left without forward movement (i.e. sideways).

10. Renvers: Performed along the wall with the horse's tail towards wall, head and body inwards at angle of forty-five degrees. Proceeding on two tracks, jaw flexed in direction of movement.

Lateral Work II

Once a young horse has been brought to work in straight lines, he is then ready to learn to move away from the rider's legs. You may work your horse on a lunge (fifteen to twenty metres) circle to obtain an initial lateral bend followed by work on serpentines and figures of eight at walk and trot. All of these movements help to supple and balance a horse. I usually start off by doing them with the horse in a long outline so as to maximise the stretching of the horse's muscles.

To commence 'true' lateral work I would start with *lateral flexions.* Position the horse at halt either alongside the wall or on the centre of the arena. Keeping the horse still with the legs, use the inside opening rein gently to relax the jaws and move the tongue in the horse's mouth. Ask him to bring his head round as far as he will without trying to move his body – this may be only one inch (2.5cm) to start with. Then straighten the horse's head and neck and try on the other rein. Let the horse stretch his neck to relieve the neck muscles as a reward. Start off with a balanced halt and an uncollected (i.e. not too high) head carriage. The lateral flexions can be practised in a collected position at a later stage. The lateral flexions help to create a relaxed jaw and supple neck muscles.

The turn on the forehand comes next and this is used to indicate to the horse to move his hind end to the side and to supple the lumbar and quarter muscles. The movement has been criticised as causing fetlock damage, but this only happens if the movement is carried out incorrectly with the front feet pivoting round without being picked up and replaced regularly. Place the horse alongside the wall, just a little way off the track. Then ask the horse to move one hind leg (the inside one) and then the other one until the horse faces the wall. This is a quarter turn on the forehand. Use your reins judiciously to help turn the forehand. Later on, a half turn can be asked for and later still (on a central line) a full turn in either direction. When stopping the movement relax your acting (inside leg) and close your outside leg immediately. The amount of leg aid used will depend upon the sensitivity of a particular horse.

The pirouette at walk can be introduced at this stage, although the most important lateral work emanating from this movement is the advanced pirouette at canter. There is also the pirouette in piaffer, a highly collected and balanced movement. However the primary use of the pirouette at walk is to supple the horse's shoulders and forehand. It is a relatively simple movement whereby the horse's forehand circles the hindquarters. The criteria is that the horse must move his hind legs in the rhythm of the walk on a very small circle, not pivoting round or stepping back. One can and should introduce the diagonal aids here. The rider's weight should be central, whilst glancing in the direction of the movement. Position the horse along the wall (a help in preventing any stepping backwards). Keeping the horse mobile but on a very small circle with the rider's legs, keep the outside leg as the acting one, whilst flexing the horse with the inside rein and using a slight opening rein, ask the horse to make a quarter turn and then halt. Build up to a half turn, and later still on the centre line ask for a full turn.

This is where the canter and pirouette comes in. When the horse is ready for collection at canter and does an easy walk to canter transition, do a pirouette at walk and pick up canter pirouette straight out of the walk. Ask for a few steps at canter and try to maintain rhythm, back into walk, keep the horse collected for a few strides and relax, and reward. Some horses will try and go into a four time rhythm, particularly the Iberians as they find it easier that way. The canter pirouette can be obtained via the canter half-pass. In both cases the horse is already in a preparatory position. The aids for the canter pirouette are diagonal, but it is important to keep the horse's balance by judicious use of the outside rein (the balancing). The rider's weight should be central but may be slightly to the outside.

Olympic gold medal winner Leslie Law and Shear L'Eau at shoulder-in at the 2004 Olympics (KIT HOUGHTON)

Shoulder-in – ten metres into and out of the movement

Pirouette in piaffer is one of the most sought after movements in High School, whereby a horse is thoroughly balanced and collected in piaffer, and then makes a full pirouette maintaining a perfect position.

As the horse becomes familiar with the previous work this is the time to start *shoulder-out* and *shoulder-in*. In the previous movements the horse has been kept nearly at a halt moving only specified limbs when asked. The halt creates a quiet atmosphere so that the horse can concentrate without being alarmed. The walk is also a good introductory pace for the same reason, but just a little more advanced. This is the pace which I would use to introduce first shoulder-out and then shoulder-in.

Introduce shoulder-out before shoulder-in as a preparatory movement. Position the horse with his face to the wall, the body being at an angle of forty-five degrees. Flex the jaw away from the direction of movement, ask the horse to move away from your leg – used on the same side as the flexion (lateral aids) and ask the horse to walk on in the position of shoulder-out, i.e. on three tracks along the wall. Just a few steps to start with. The rider's body weight should be central with the rider looking in the direction of the movement. Straighten the outside rein to bring the horse out of shoulder-out or shoulder-in.

Shoulder-in is a bit more difficult because you do not have the wall to stop the horse advancing forwards. Again start off in walk, the trot should only be introduced once the horse is proficient and confident at the walk. Position the horse at an angle of forty-five degrees facing into the arena, flex the jaw away from the direction of movement, ask the horse to move away from your leg – the leg on the same side as the flexion (lateral aids). The rider's body weight is central with the rider glancing in the direction of movement. Ask the horse to move on three tracks – along the wall to start with – just a few paces. Build up to more steps and then try a trot. The more supple and balanced the horse becomes the easier he will find the movement. When coming out of the shoulder-in it is an idea to ride a ten to fifteen metre circle and on meeting the wall again to then go straight. In the trot the circle may be fifteen to twenty metres. The volte (eight metres) comes later.

Each of the lateral movements has its own degree of difficulty. By proceeding logically one can reduce the problems involved. Before teaching the half-pass leg yielding is an excellent preparatory exercise. It is performed on two tracks and although the horse looks away from the direction of movement, I personally have not encountered any difficulty in teaching the horse a half-pass where the bend is in the direction of the movement. If the horse were to refuse to look in the correct direction in half-pass I would consider either that the horse was not properly prepared (i.e. stiff) or that there was a rider problem.

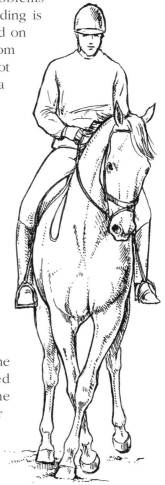

Leg yielding is a good disciplinary and suppling exercise working both ends of the horse. The front and hind legs each follow a separate track crossing over (front over front, hind over hind), with the horse flexed away from the direction of movement. The aids are lateral, the inside acting leg and inside hand using the opening rein, the rider's weight central but following the horse's leading shoulder. I like to turn the horse up the centre line and with my inside leg ask him to proceed forward and sideways back to the side of the arena. Leg yielding can be performed at walk or trot, but remember it is quite severe on the muscles, so don't do too much at a time.

Travers is another introduction to the half-pass. It is performed along the wall. Position the horse with his head to the wall at an angle

Leg yielding (to the right)

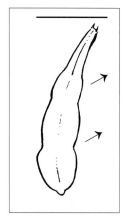

Travers
(head to wall)

of forty-five degrees. Flex the jaw in the direction of the movement, ask the horse to move away from your outside leg. The aids are diagonal and the horse should move on two tracks. The rider's body is central but following the horse's movement, the rider glancing in the direction of the movement. This movement is often used to improve suppleness, the crossing of the horse's legs and the bend.

This is one of the first movements where the diagonal or collecting aids are used for the lateral movements. The horse is required to bend evenly from head to tail in travers, whereas the horse's body is straighter in leg yielding.

The *half-pass* is when the horse advances diagonally across the arena making two tracks. The horse gains some ground forwards and some sideways hence the name half-pass. A horse needs to be well balanced, supple and to a degree collected before attempting to half-pass. To free the horse's shoulders so as to allow the horse to move and look in the direction of movement he has to carry his neck quite high. If the neck is pulled up the horse will hollow his back and if uncollected (i.e. with a low head carriage) he will be on his forehand and probably look away from the direction in which he is moving as in leg yielding. It is logical therefore, that a certain degree of schooling is necessary.

Half-pass

Positioning is important. Place the horse along the wall as if for shoulder-in, but instead of using as your acting leg µyour inside one, use the opposite (outside) one. Sometimes to make sure the bend and position are correct, do one stride of shoulder-in and then reverse the leg aids, thence movement into the arena not along the wall.

The rein aids are important. Keep your outside rein close to the horse's neck, whilst your inside rein (opening rein) will ask for the flexion and guide the horse's forehand in the direction of the movement of the horse's leading shoulder. The rider's hips and back must be supple – any stiffening of the rider's body will cause resistance. Look between your horse's ears, and be able at the same time to see the ball of your horse's eye – no more. Teach the horse the movement at walk and later at trot and canter.

The *counter change of hand* at canter is when the horse moves from right to left or vice versa in half-pass and is asked for in various Advanced dressage tests. The actual change causes a good deal of discussion as does the amount of bend required. Some judges want a change of bend with no straight stride in between bends and others do not allow this. With a young or stiff horse a straight stride makes things easier because horse and rider have time to adjust, whereas with no straightening the horse needs to be very supple and well balanced. In the counter change of hand with a flying change you need a straight, well balanced horse with not as much bend as in the trot where the cross over is very important. Being in two time, this can be shown to a greater extent with the bend well emphasised as well as the degree of collection.

The rider needs to harmonise the leg aids and the hand (rein) aids making the transition from one bend to the next subtle and smooth. The timing of the application of the 'new' aids is vital to the successful change. A late or mis-timed aid can cause disaster.

A dressage judge will assess the quality of the half-passes and counter changes of hand by the degree of elegance, together with the rhythm, balance and suppleness plus the correct bend.

Renvers is the most difficult of the lateral training exercises. It requires a very supple, obedient horse. Position the horse at an angle of forty-five degrees facing into the arena, the tail to the wall. Flex the horse with an opening rein to face in the direction of movement, use the leg on the opposite side to the flexion to ask him to move to the side on two tracks. The rider's body must be

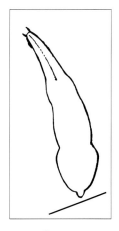

*Renvers
to the right (tail to
wall)*

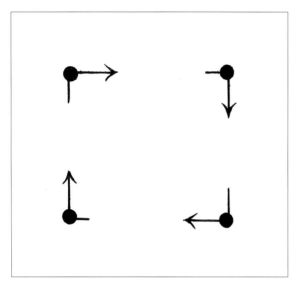

central and the rider glancing in the direction of the movement. As in travers the horse should be evenly bent from head to tail, crossing his legs over with emphasis. Ask for this movement in walk and later when confident, at trot.

The *full pass* is not asked for in ordinary dressage competitions, but is asked for in Police

The square

● = *Horse's hooves*

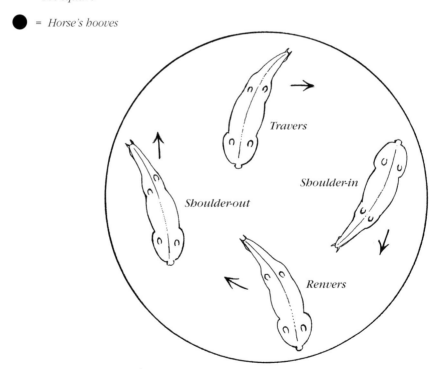

The circle

Horse Competitions and in the Spanish Doma Vacquera. It is used by Military horses on parade to move to the side without having to break rank. The horse moves to the side without gaining ground to the front, hence the term full pass. In most cases the horse is being ridden with one hand – the rein being in the left hand (the bridle hand) leaving the right hand free. The horse is asked to move to the side by use of the rider's leg and body weight. This use of body and leg aids must be practically invisible, the rider remaining in an upright position.

Aids for Lateral Movements

Lateral Movements with Lateral Aids

1. Turn on forehand
2. Large circle (twenty metres)
3. Serpentine
4. Using corner make full circle (ten to twelve metres)
5. Shoulder-out
6. Leg yielding
7. Shoulder-in

Lateral Movements with Diagonal Aids

1. Turn on forehand (stop horse with outside leg)
2. Pirouette at walk (i.e. turn on hindquarters)
3. Travers
4. Renvers
5. Half-pass

Two Special Exercises

1. The Square:
   Half pirouette at walk at four corners of square. Used by de la Gueriniere to collect a horse, and eventually reducing the square to a central point where the horse performs a full pirouette.
2. The Circle:
   Shoulder-Out – Travers – Shoulder-In – Renvers
   A quarter of the circle in each movement; the circle is approximately ten metres. To be performed at walk only.

Sequence of Progression

Today both the training methods and the horses used for dressage are built around the European Warmblood or Sport Horse.

One should, therefore, have a programme and a set target. The programme can be built around the two criteria of straight line and lateral work, with collection and extension as further basic points. If we add to these the essentials of developing suppleness, instilling obedience and maintaining calmness, things should not go far wrong. Further to this, there is no doubt that, even though all horses are slightly different, correct development and suppling of the muscles will lead to easier performance of the next exercise. This is not wholly a physical matter; if correct muscular development makes it easier for a horse to perform a movement, he is more likely to remain calm and obedient whilst doing so.

The next point to consider is the immediate progression within a given movement; giving the horse a position, asking him through the aids and then allowing him to perform the movement requested – a classical and essentially simple formula which sometimes seems easier said than done.

Having, then, established these principles, we next have to consider the detail of what work to ask for, and in what sequence. I have set out below a sequence of exercises which, carried out correctly, should produce a well schooled horse.

Basic Exercises

1) Walk the horse in straight lines.
2) Keep a feel on the outside rein and ask for slight flexion to the inside on a twenty metre circle.
3) Transitions halt to walk, walk to trot and vice versa.
4) Through corners with slight flexion to the inside.
5) Changes of rein with correct flexions at walk and then trot.
6) Shoulder-in position at walk.
7) Shoulder-out and shoulder-in.
8) Correct halt.
9) Rein-back.
10) Further upward and downward transitions, with accent on correct positions.

11) Collection and extension at trot.
12) Canter from walk.

Lateral Work (Progression from 7)

13) Shoulder-in to travers and vice versa.
14) Shoulder-out to renvers and vice versa.
15) Shoulder-in to renvers and vice versa.
16) Shoulder-out to travers and vice versa.
17) Shoulder-in to shoulder-out and vice versa.
18) Travers to renvers and vice versa.
19) Small (fifteen metre) circles incorporating various combinations of the above exercises.

Canter Work

20) Correct strike off at canter on a circle. To begin with, this can be from a balanced trot, but should then be practised from walk.
21) Medium canter.
22) Collected canter.
23) Travers at canter.
24) Pirouette at canter.
25) Figure-of-eight at canter, with simple change of leg.
26) Figure-of-eight at canter with flying change.
27) Changes of lead every six strides, progressing gradually towards one-time changes (on a straight line).

Passage and Piaffer

28) Work on increasing engagement and elevation of hind legs.
29) First steps of piaffer.
30) Consolidating piaffer.
31) Passage from either walk or trot.

The author on the Thoroughbred Le Marquis in piaffer, showing good balance. The rider is using a reasonably strong seat (FIONA FORBES)

10.
ADVANCED

Piaffer

When a rider or horse gets to the standard of piaffer and passage they will undoubtedly need help from a trainer who understands this highly collected work. It is really no good trying to take these movements out of context. The horse should be properly prepared (via the previous programme) and positioned along a straight part of the training area facing left.

Most trainers prefer to teach the horse the piaffer before the passage. There are many ways to teach this movement. Some trainers like to do it from the ground (dismounted). Certainly a trainer working alongside the rider will be a big help.

The horse must learn to shorten and heighten his stride at the walk to start, and then at the trot until he is in effect marking time on the spot, or very nearly so. The first steps may be tentative, and should be accepted. Only when the horse is calm should he be asked for more steps and less forward movement. This is where the person on the ground can help by touching the horse's legs (front and back) lightly with a schooling whip to encourage him to pick up his legs. The rider keeps leg pressure on and an even, but light, contact on the reins, sitting in an upright position to help the horse keep his balance.

The piaffer is in reality the trot on the spot and it is done in a rhythm of two time. With the shortened base, the horse's neck is raised with the muzzle at, or nearly at, withers level. The hind legs come up further under the horse's body, thus carrying more weight and lightening the front end. This is a time when a rider can benefit from the feel of this high collection on a trained horse.

The piaffer is the preparation for many of the High School's Airs. The transitions from piaffer to other movements are marked very highly in dressage tests where the movement is included (Prix St Georges and above). The piaffer can be asked for in either a snaffle or double bridle, the latter is

Anika van Grunsven on Salinero demonstrates excellent balance and co-ordination in passage (KIT HOUGHTON)

mandatory in a test. Some horses are not capable of attaining this high standard because of conformation, age or temperament. Like all collected movements, start by applying the legs and then start to half-halt, with the hands raising (but never pulling) the reins upwards about three to four inches (7.6 or 10cm) gradually. It may take several weeks to establish the movement. Don't hurry it! Two steps, three, four and on upwards to a dozen or more.

The Passage

Probably the passage, that highly elevated trot, is one of the most spectacular of all the dressage movements. It is not easily obtained, although nearly all horses will perform it loose if excited by something, but obtaining to order is another thing. Like the piaffer it must be put in context and prepared through the proper programme. Some horses may be ready in about two years, others never get there. The ability to obtain a good passage lies in the horse having naturally good balance and a certain amount of knee action. The Thoroughbred finds it the most difficult movement, but can do it, whereas a Warmblood or Andalusian finds it relatively easy, but then the Thoroughbred can extend more easily, so choice of a horse is important if you really want to do Grand Prix dressage.

A lesson, or lessons on a schoolmaster will be a necessity. The feel of a real passage is very special.

Lough Thorn – Dublin Hunter Champion
(CHARLES C FENNELL)

11.
MISCELLANEOUS

Uses of a Schoolmaster

As I have said in chapter 4 on 'Introduction to Balance', you do not always need a fancy schoolmaster. However, if the rider is really serious, a schoolmaster can be very useful. It is not necessary to own one, really rather better to have a lesson on a trained horse for a specific purpose. Schoolmasters – or good ones at any rate – should be good at one or two particular movements, such as lateral work, collection or flying changes for example. Most good riding schools have horses that they keep for private lessons on specialised subjects.

A schoolmaster should *not* be an 'all rounder' on anything and everything, nor should it be a failed horse that, for instance, bucks or naps continually. A good schoolmaster is worth his weight in gold – being a specialist at his job.

To sit on a horse that collects well will give the rider the feel of the arching of the neck and the correct balance of the horse. One that can give the difference in the feel of the medium and extended trots is invaluable and so it goes on.

In the old days a cavalry officer, once he had learned to ride a trained horse, was then allocated a trained horse, a semi-trained horse and an

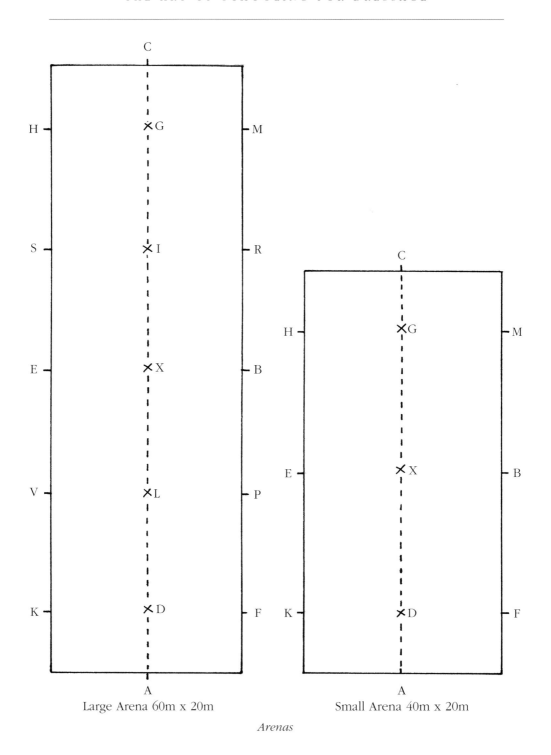

Large Arena 60m x 20m   Small Arena 40m x 20m

Arenas

untrained one. So today's schoolmaster is the equivalent of the trained horse; i.e. he teaches the rider. Another thing a schoolmaster (or trained horse) can do is to teach the rider rhythm.

Analysis of a Dressage Test

Dressage tests are divided into standards, starting with Preliminary and Working and going through Novice, Medium and Prix St Georges to Grand Prix. These tests not only contain movements but the judge will look for quality of movement, balance, suppleness and accuracy. Horses have to qualify for the higher grades.

When training a horse for a certain test I like to analyse the transitions as well as the movements required. The movements for, say, a Novice test carried out at Working level require the balance and suppleness required in a young horse, whereas a test at Grand Prix level requires much more collection and fuller extensions. This work is time consuming and needs patience, you cannot take movements (successfully) out of context.

Preliminary

Movements: Straight lines, changes of direction, turns, circles twenty metres.

Transitions: Walk – trot, trot to canter, canter – trot, trot to walk.
All at Working Level

Novice

Movements: As above plus half circles.

Transitions: All at working plus a few strides medium trot.
All at Novice Level

Elementary

Movements: As above but smaller circles (ten metres). Simple change of leg at canter and rein back.

Transitions: As above but including medium trot, medium canter and some collected trot and lateral work (shoulder-in).
All at Elementary Level

Medium

> Movements: As above, but including half-pass (at trot) and half-pirouette
> at walk.
> Transitions: Medium paces and some collection.

Prix St Georges

Movements and transition at Collected and Extended Level. Half-pirouettes at canter, flying changes, full extended trot, piaffer.

Grand Prix

Piaffer, passage, one and two time changes, highly marked transitions.

Work with Cavalletti

Cavalletti are useful to improve balance and suppleness. They are particularly helpful in suppling and developing the muscles along the horse's back and neck. Horses can be worked over cavalletti very beneficially at either the walk or the gait best suited to working horses – the

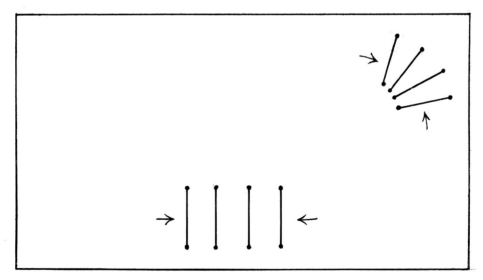

Cavalletti

trot. It is easiest to work over a set of four cavalletti, and they can be used at all stages of training.

The spacing between cavalletti will vary according to the work of the day, the level of training of the horse, and his natural length of stride. When introducing cavalletti via walk, the spacing should be in the order of 0.8 to 0.9m (2ft 9in to 3ft). For ordinary trot work, a distance of about 1.3m (4 ft 6in) is a fair starting point for most horses. In due course, collection and extension can both be practised. Spacing can be brought in to about 0.9m (3ft) for collected trot and brought out to 1.55m (5ft) or more for extended trot. However, it is important to start with the spacing easiest for the horse's work by degrees.

The height of the cavelletti is usually about 10 to 15cm (4 to 6in) on their lowest setting and 23 to 30cm (9 to12in) on their highest. I prefer to set them low to begin with, to avoid injury to the horse's legs (which can, of course, be booted or bandaged) or to the muscles of his back. Remember that muscles can very easily be damaged if worked beyond their capacity. It is the job of the trainer to develop, not destroy, muscles and, for that matter, to seek the horse's co-operation, rather than frightening him.

The cavalletti can be placed either alongside the wall of the school or, if the horse is unlikely to run out, on a straight line in the centre of a wide school. In the latter position, they can be approached readily on either rein from either direction. A further setting is to place them on a circle, taking care that the curve of the set of cavalletti corresponds to the curve of the circle. With this setting it is possible, as the horse progresses, to ask for slightly longer or shorter strides by moving the horse a little towards the outside or inside of the cavalletti, respectively.

Nicky Herbert showing the correct seat on Sandal, a Thoroughbred/Argentinian cross bred by HM The Queen. This horse worked for many years with the Horse Rangers Association.

12.
CONCLUSION

If you have had the patience to read through the various chapters of this book I would like to make a few comments.

The chapters are logical and they do work, but they are only guidelines. It is *how* you use them that really counts. There are some things you cannot explain by writing them down. You can learn to *feel* what is right or wrong and if you have an instructor, that person can often *see* what the problem is.

I well remember riding a very highly schooled horse called 'Gay Rowland' and was endeavouring to achieve a demi-piroutte at walk. Everything was going wrong and I was using more and more aid. Mr Schmit Jensen came into the school and asked what the matter was; to which I replied that I was using stronger and stronger aids. 'Oh, he said, don't use any aids, just look round' and of course the horse responded immediately. He was a sensitive, intelligent horse, and being highly trained he only needed an indication.

Another mis-conception I come up against is riders trying to hold up a horse's head, or as they see it 'fixing' the head or even flexing the jaw. You cannot hold up a horse's head and anyway he needs a free head to balance himself. You can however, school to develop the crest (top neck) muscles so that the horse can carry his own head.

We had, when I was at Burton Hall, several horses that could be ridden without bridle (the famous 'Korbous', Wembley 1964) was one; 'Sea Lion' and 'K & P' others. The idea being to show the rider's body position organised the horse *not* the reins.

Music is something I haven't said anything about. In the Musical Kür the rider has to think of *rhythm*. Rhythm is important, *but* to me *inspiration* is what I like music for. It seems to me that the musicians never make mistakes and it is up to me to ride better. The feeling for me of a lovely Thoroughbred responding nicely to my aids with a background of Beethoven or Mozart is out of this world – yes, a lovely Iberian will do!

I think one of the most difficult things is when, on one's own, a problem occurs, and one just simply cannot solve it. One useful idea is to stop doing the movement that is causing trouble and try something you know the horse likes to do and then the next day try the difficult one again. It may be that the horse is simply not ready to do the difficult movement.

There are some horses who simply don't have the ability to perform certain movements, others have pain somewhere and others have been ruined along the way. Schooling is complex, but it wouldn't the fun it is if it wasn't.

The author on her mare Fanny showing a good working canter and correct seat.
(CHARLES FENNELL)

INDEX

(*numbers in italics refer to illustrations*)